Extended Life CTM

GOT A LIFE?
It's Your Gift from God

A Bible study that examines the subject of
being spiritually born again

Karen E. Connell

ISBN-13:978-1489575890
ISBN-10:1489575898

Published by: Extended Life Christian Training Ministry, Inc.,
Houghton, Michigan, All Rights Reserved
Copyright © Revised 2016, First Edition 2005

Permission is granted to publish all or parts of this book for distribution as long as it is don free of charge. However, this book may not be reprinted or placed on the internet without express permission from the author.

Bible quotes are from several Bible versions. The particular Bible version is indicated by the following abbreviations.

KJV	The King James Version of the Bible.
NIV	The Holy Bible, New International Version. Copyright 1973, 1978, 1984, by the International Bible Society. All Rights Reserved.
NLT	New Living Translation Bible. Copyright THE LOCKMAN FOUNDATION, 1960, 1962, 1963, 1968, 1971, 1973, 1975, 1977. A corporation not for profit. La Habra, California. All Rights Reserved
AMP	The Amplified Bible. Copyright by Zondervan Publishing House, 1965, Grand Rapids, Michigan. All Rights Reserved.

Word studies and definitions are from several sources.
The particular source is indicated by the following abbreviations.

STR	Biblesoft's New Exhaustive Strong's Numbers and Concordance With Expanded Greek and Hebrew Dictionary. Copyright © 1994 Biblesoft & International Bible Translators, Inc. All Rights Reserved
THAY	Thayer's Greek Lexicon (Complete and Abridged Formats) Electronic Database. Copyright © 2000 by Biblesoft and International Bible Translators, Inc. All Rights Reserved
B/D/B	Brown-Driver &Briggs Hebrew Lexicon, Copyright © 1993 Woodside Bible Fellowship, Ontario, Canada, Licensed from the Institute for Creation research. All Rights Reserved
CWSD	Complete Word Studies Dictionary © 1992 by AMG International, Inc.

DEDICATION

This book is dedicated to all those who are serious about fulfilling the eternal destiny that our Heavenly Father ordained before the foundation of the world, for those who choose to follow Jesus Christ as a true disciple.

EXTENDED LIFE C.T.M. Publishing
ExtendedlifeCTM.org

Extended_life@hotmail.com

APPRECIATION

I am blessed and thankful for the loving encouragement, the love of my life, my husband Garry, has given me, in helping to put this book in the hands of those wanting God's gift

Jesus said...

I am the door. Those who come in through me will be saved. Wherever they go, they will find green pastures...

My purpose is to give life in all its fullness.

John 10:9-10

Table of Contents

PREFACE 10

CHAPTER 1 15

NEW BIRTH—NEW LIFE! 15

    JESUS SAID WE MUST BE BORN AGAIN! 16
    HOW DO WE GET THE LIGHT OF LIFE FROM GOD? 18
        We are All in the Same Boat 20
        Jesus Christ is God 23
        True Faith 27
    WE CAN KNOW FOR SURE THAT WE ARE BORN AGAIN 28
    A PRAYER OF REPENTANCE 28
    YOU HAVE A GLORIOUS ETERNAL DESTINY 30

.... 32

CHAPTER 2 32

    COUNTING THE COST 32
.... 35
    THE COST OF TRUE DISCIPLESHIP 35
    THE REWARDS OF DISCIPLESHIP 39
        We Are Justified 42
        Quenching God's Holy Spirit 43

.... 45

CHAPTER 3 45

GROWING IN THE NEW LIFE 45

    YOU MUST BE WATER BAPTIZED 48
        When Christians Backslide 56
        The Abundant life is Doing What Jesus Did! 61
    YOU MUST BE BAPTIZED WITH THE   HOLY SPIRIT 64
    SPIRITUAL GIFTS 70
    RECEIVING THE BAPTISM OF THE HOLY SPIRIT 72
        Speaking Gift Activation Prayer 75
    BECOME A SANCTIFIED BELIEVER 76

- THE GLORIFIED SAINTS 77
  - *Being Prepared for the End-Times* 83
- FIND A BIBLE BELIEVING FELLOWSHIP 88
  - *Understanding the Body of Christ* 90
- DEVELOP A DAILY BIBLE STUDY PLAN 92
  - *The Holy Spirit is and Must Be Your Teacher* 93
- TAKE TIME TO PRAY 98

CHAPTER 4 105

THE BIBLE 105

- THE ACCURACY OF THE BIBLE 108
- THE INSPIRATION OF THE BIBLE 109

Preface

"My Story"

For I know the plans I have for you," says the LORD. "They are plans for good and not for disaster, to give you a future and a hope...In those days when you pray, I will listen...If you look for me in earnest, you will find me when you seek me... I will be found by you," says the LORD. (Jeremiah 29:11-14) NLT

You may be like I once was—tired of the life you are now living and would welcome the idea of having *a new life* and a chance to start all over again. If so, keep reading this booklet. My prayer is that you will discover, as I did, how to receive God's gift of *eternal life.* This gift is given to all who put their faith in Jesus Christ, for He is the only way to obtain this new life. Jesus Himself claimed to be THE only way to find truth and life.

For the wages of sin is death; but <u>the gift of God is eternal life</u> through Jesus Christ our Lord. (Romans 6:23) KJV

Jesus told him, "I am <u>the </u>way, <u>the </u>truth, and <u>the </u>life. (John 14:6) KJV

There is no other religion, god or philosophy anywhere on this earth, that can change the sinful, shame and guilt filled nature of a human being. It is an undeniable fact that every person born on this earth has a sinful nature that produces wrong thoughts, attitudes and actions called sin. No one can escape this fact.

The Bible tells us Jesus Christ, as God—came to earth and took on the form of a human being. He then suffered the pangs of death and rose again from the dead. His death, burial and resurrection purchased for us God's gift of eternal life, which is now freely offered to all who will receive salvation from their sin through faith in   Jesus Christ.

As he [Joseph] considered this, he fell asleep, and an angel of the Lord appeared to him in a dream. "Joseph, son of David," the angel said, "do not be afraid to go ahead with your marriage to Mary. For <u>the child within her has been conceived by the Holy Spirit</u>... And she will have a son, and you are to name him Jesus, for <u>he will save his people from their sins</u>." (Matthew 1:20-21)

Jesus Christ was the first human being to ever possess God's very own life or nature living within Him. The Bible tells us that others would become related to Him, by being *born again spiritually*.

God chose us to become like his Son, so that his Son would be the firstborn, with many brothers and sisters. (Romans 8:29)

In order to become a brother or sister to Jesus Christ we must be born spiritually into His family. This booklet will share how this is possible. Many, like myself before my new birth, are living in a place of feeling hopeless and helpless. For those in this place—there truly is *Good News* to be found within these pages.

I'll never forget the day I found out that God was offering me an opportunity to start my life all over again with Him. Up to that time I had pretty much believed that God had written me off. The reason this was the case was because when I was 14 years old I receive Jesus Christ as my personal Savior. However, by the time I had turned 16, other things began to take control of my life, and like the prodigal son, in (Luke 15:11-32), I chose to walk away from God and retreat back into a life of sin by living life—MY WAY—and not God's way.

Somewhere along the way I came to believe Satan's lie that I had blown my chance with God—and as a result I struggled with deep insecurity, guilt, and shame because of my sinful life. This drove me further away from God and into a never ending quest for something to make me happy.

By the age of 21 I was becoming dependent upon alcohol as a means of trying to escape the misery and the depression I was living in. Then one day a local pastor knocked on my door and began telling me I could start all over again with God. He read verses from his Bible which told me how much God loved me *despite my sin*, and that He was willing to forgive me and totally accept me. I was more than ready at that point in my life to receive this *Good News* called—the gospel! This time, I was willing to not only receive Jesus as my Savior from all my sin, but now I was willing to make Him the *Lord of my life*. That day, about a week before my 21st birthday, I finally *got a life!* I want to say that this new life is the greatest gift anyone could ever receive.

Since that time, God has made Himself known to me in a very real way— as my loving heavenly father. He has helped me to experience great freedom and healing from the painful insecurity, guilt, and shame issues that had created deep bouts of depression which plagued my life for so long.

Before becoming a *true Christian*, I found out that following a *religion* or *any self-help philosophy* could not change me or my painful circumstances. Like so many sincere people, who don't have a personal relationship with God through faith in Jesus Christ, I tried to be a *good person*. I tried to better myself in order to change what I didn't like about my life. But none of these things could change my sinful self-centeredness, anger and prideful ways. No wonder God says to us...

Can the Ethiopian change his skin or the leopard its spots? Neither can you do good who are accustomed to doing evil. (Jeremiah 13:23)

I thank God for bringing me the truth, which is—It doesn't matter what church you attend, or how many *religious good works* you do in order to please God, we can only come to know Him and be accepted by Him through repenting of our sin and being born into His family.

This booklet will explain what the Bible teaches on how this is possible. Without experiencing this new spiritual birth, we will continue to struggle with trying to knowing God on a personal level. Without a personal relationship with the true and living God, we will not have the assurance and peace of knowing we have *eternal life*. We are all going to face death at some point and the only access into eternal life and being saved from eternal damnation—is through being born-again by faith in Jesus Christ.

Put all your rebellion behind you, and get for yourselves a new heart and a new spirit... Turn back to Me and live! (Ezekiel 18:31-32) NLT

God wants every person on planet earth to know that we truly can have a *NEW and eternal life* through faith in Jesus Christ. The wonderful promise from God is that He will make all things new— no matter how old, how young or how messed up a life may be. This was the Good News I longed to hear and it came at a very low point in my life.

Therefore, if any man be in Christ, he is a new creature: old things are passed away; behold, all things become new. (2 Corinthians 5:17) NJKV

Maybe your life is not all messed up like mine was and you may you think you're a pretty good person and believe your life is just fine without God. Those who feel this way fail to realize that one day, as the Bible states—every person who has ever lived on planet earth is

going to stand before the Most-High God of this universe to be judged by Him. It really doesn't matter if you believe this or not—just rest assured and be forewarned—it is going to happen!

Then I saw a great white throne and Him who sat on it... And I saw the dead, small and great, standing before God, and books were opened. And another book was opened, which is the <u>Book of Life</u>. And the dead were judged according to their works, by the things which were written in the books. (Revelation 20:11) NKJV

The Bible is clear about the fact that *every person* has an appointment with death—and this is one appointment we will all keep.

It is appointed for men to die once, and after this the judgment. (Hebrews 9:27) NKJV

I no longer have to fear what will happen to me after I keep my appointment with death, because *I know* my name is now written in God's *Book of Life*. The Bible promises that those who have received new life from God through faith in Jesus Christ—will have their names written in His *Book of Life*. This means they will be saved from the punishment of being sentenced for eternity to a horrible place known as *the Lake of Fire*.

The devil, who deceived them, was cast into the lake of fire and brimstone where the beast and the false prophet are. And they will be tormented day and night forever and ever... And anyone not found written in the Book of Life was cast into the lake of fire. (Revelation 20:10, 15) NKJV

My prayer is that you will carefully and prayerfully consider what you are about to read. You will not only learn what you need to know about how to truly change your present life—but even more importantly what is contained in the pages of this book may ultimately well determine your *eternal* destiny.

CHAPTER 1

New Birth—New Life!

My new life began the day *my spirit* gained light or life from God. The Bible says every person needs new life by being born-again. Why? Because until we are born again we are spiritually (dead) separated from God because of our sin. This makes it impossible for us to have a personal relationship with God. Without being *born again* God is not a reality in our lives. We may believe He exists, and learn many things about Him, but that's as far as we can go in our experience with Him—unless we are born again. One of the reasons God created human beings was so He could have a loving relationship with them. The Bible says that Adam and Eve, the first humans created by God, had this kind of intimate relationship with Him—before they sinned.

And they (Adam and Eve) **heard the voice of the LORD God walking in the garden in the cool of the day...And the LORD God called unto Adam, and said unto him, <u>where are you</u>? (Genesis 3:8-9)**

This verse shows us God's desire to have fellowship with Adam and Eve. This story goes on to say that God's arch enemy, Satan, was also in that garden and spoke to them enticing them and tricking them into <u>mistrusting their God</u> who loved them.

Unfortunately, they chose to believe Satan instead of God. This allowed sin to enter their lives and the lives of every human born from that point on. This means we inherited a human nature that has the tendency to believe Satan and to mistrust God. <u>This is the root for all sin</u>. The Bible calls this inherited tendency *iniquity*.

...for I the LORD thy God am a jealous God, visiting the <u>iniquity of the fathers</u> upon the children unto the third and fourth generation of them that hate me... (Exodus 20:5) KJV

You might say, "I don't hate God." The truth is—we either love Him or hate Him. God says if we love Him we honor Him by desiring to obey His Word. When we don't care about honoring God's desires, He says we *hate* Him. This literally means we are *against Him*. Jesus, who was God in the form of man said...

He that is not with me <u>is against me</u>. (Matthew 12:30) KJV

If you love me, keep my commandments. (John 14:15) KJV

Therefore, God defines love for Him as *obedience* and hate for Him as *disobedience*. As human beings it is not our nature to love God or to honor His desires. Instead we honor our own desires, which come from the world around us, our own inherited human nature, and from spiritual demonic influences.

That is why we need to be born again and receive *a new nature* that has Godly desires. This new nature comes from God's sinless seed which is conceived within us when we put our faith in Jesus Christ as our Lord and Savior.

Being born again, not of <u>corruptible seed</u>, but of incorruptible, <u>by the word of God</u>, which lives and abides forever. (1 Peter 1:23) KJV

Jesus Said We Must Be Born Again!

The first time we were born we had a physical birth. At that time as I have just explained, we received a fallen human nature that mistrusts God and is <u>bent on sinning</u>.

Sin and the guilt it produces keeps us separated from God, just as it separated Adam and Eve from God. Therefore, being born again doesn't mean we need another physical birth, but rather a spiritual birth. Jesus was trying to explain this concept to an important religious Jewish leader of His day...

There was a man of the Pharisees, named Nicodemus, a ruler of the Jews...The same came to Jesus by night, and said unto him, Rabbi, we know that thou are a teacher come from God: <u>for no man can do these miracles that thou do, except God be with him</u>....Jesus answered and said unto him, Verily, verily, I say unto thee, <u>except a man be born again</u>, he cannot see the kingdom of God...

Nicodemus said unto him, "How can a man be born when he is old? Can he enter the second time into his mother's womb, and be born?" ....Jesus answered, Verily, verily, I say unto thee, except a man be born of water and of the Spirit, he cannot enter into the kingdom of God... That which is born of the flesh is flesh; and that which is born of the Spirit is spirit. ...Marvel not that I said unto thee, <u>you must be born again</u>. (John 3:3-6) KJV

All Nicodemus knew was that Jesus was a human being who had a very close relationship with God. In fact, the Greek texts say that this man told Jesus he could see that God accompanied Him as a constant *companion.*

What Nicodemus wanted to know from Jesus, was how this close relationship or fellowship with God was possible? He could see by the miracles Jesus did that his personal relationship with God gave Him power from God. Nicodemus was a Jewish ruler, who knew all <u>about God</u>. But God wasn't "with him" like he saw demonstrated in Jesus' life.

Jesus told Nicodemus that in order to have a living vital relationship with God, he had to be born *again.* The Bible teaches us that humans have a *spirit* and a *soul* which live in a *physical* body. At the time of our physical birth, our spirit is separated from God and lives in spiritual darkness. Therefore, we can't have a personal living relationship with God— who is light. The Bible also says our human spirit is like a candle. However, not every spirit or candle has God's spiritual light or life upon it. God needs to bring His light or life upon our human spirit…

<u>The spirit of man is the candle</u> of the LORD, searching all the inward parts of the belly. (Proverbs 20:27) KJV

<u>For you will light my candle</u>: the LORD my God will enlighten my darkness. (Psalm 18:28) NKJV

There are some important points that need to be considered when it comes to understanding the born again experience.

How Do We Get the Light of Life from God?

Jesus said that He was the only *source* for the light that gives us spiritual life. Until we put our faith in this truth—we will live in spiritual darkness.

Then spoke Jesus again unto them, saying, <u>I am the light of the world</u>: he that follows me shall not walk in darkness, but shall have <u>the light of life</u>. (John 8:12) KJV

God's light and life can only come from Jesus Christ... there is no other way! There are not many ways or roads to God. Jesus Christ is the only way...

Be it known unto you all, and to all the people of Israel, that by the name of Jesus Christ of Nazareth, whom ye crucified, whom God raised from the dead, ...<u>Neither is there salvation in any other</u>: for there is no other name under heaven given among men, whereby we must be saved. (Acts 4:10-12) KJV

Jesus claimed to be God, and said that He was the only way to experience God in our life...

I and my Father <u>are one</u> (literally in the Greek this means: "one and the same"). (John 10:30) KJV

I am the way, the truth, and the life: no man cometh unto the Father, but by me. (John 14:6) KJV

And without controversy great is the mystery of godliness: God was manifest in the flesh (as Jesus Christ). **(1 Timothy 3:16) KJV** (Parenthesis mine).

SIN SEPARATES People FROM GOD   Receive   To be with   God
Jesus Christ

Therefore, until we put our faith in Jesus Christ as our Lord and Savior, we will remain spiritually dead. You can read the account in Genesis chapter three, which explains how the first created humans sinned.

God warned them if they disobeyed Him <u>they would die</u>. He didn't mean they would physically drop dead on the spot, because Adam lived 930 more years after he sinned. It was, however, an instant spiritual death that took place—causing them to be separated from God.

From that time until now, all who are born into this world, are born into sin and remain separated from God by their inherited sin nature from Adam.

Therefore, just as sin entered the world through one man (Adam) and death through sin, and in this way death came to all men, because all sinned— (Romans 5:12) NIV

We are All in the Same Boat

Those without Jesus Christ are like those on a sinking boat called SIN, and it is taking them right down to eternal destruction! We are all born with the desire to sin—separated from God and possessing a fallen human nature that does not trust God nor desires to honor Him.

For <u>all have sinned</u>, and come short of the glory of God; (Romans 3:23) KJV

There is no other reason than pride, for us not to confess we are a sinner—in need of a Savior. God has put within every human being a *conscience* that accuses us of our wrong doing—plainly letting us know we are sinners…

…in their hearts those who don't know God, do know right from wrong…They demonstrate that God's law is written within them, for <u>their own consciences either accuse them</u> or tells them they are doing what is right…The day will surely come when God, by Jesus Christ, will judge everyone's secret life. (Romans 2:14-16) NLT

In the same way no person can say they don't believe God exists. The Bible says God has put a measure of faith in the hearts of all people so they can find Him if they so desire.

...think soberly, according as God hath dealt to every man the measure of faith. (Romans 12:3) KJV

We however, have to make the decision to use the measure of faith that God has placed within every person. We will find God if we turn to Him and seek Him for ourselves...

For I know the plans I have for you," says the LORD. "They are plans for good and not for disaster, to give you a future and a hope...In those days when you pray, I will listen... If you look for me in earnest, you will find me when you seek me... I will be found by you," says the LORD. (Jeremiah 29:11-14) NLT

God doesn't want to see anyone die and spend eternity in hell. On the other hand, it is not God's fault that people end up in hell, because anyone who dies and goes to hell simply *did not take the time to search for God* and receive what Jesus died to give them.

Those who seek after God and want to know Him *will find Him*. Jesus promised to reveal Himself to those who want to find God...

I will love him, and will manifest myself to him. (John 14:21) KJV

If you look for me in earnest, you will find me when you seek me... I will be found by you," says the LORD. (Jer 29:13-14) NLT

DO YOUR OWN THING AND ... in the end it will lead you straight to Hell!

"there is a way that seems right to a man, but it ends in the way to death" Proverbs 16:25

Every time we refuse to pay attention to the word of God when it comes to us, we are ignoring **the measure of faith** within us. There were so many times I refused to listen to those who spoke of God and the Bible. I didn't want to hear it! Like Adam and Eve in the Garden of Eden, I too was running and hiding from God.

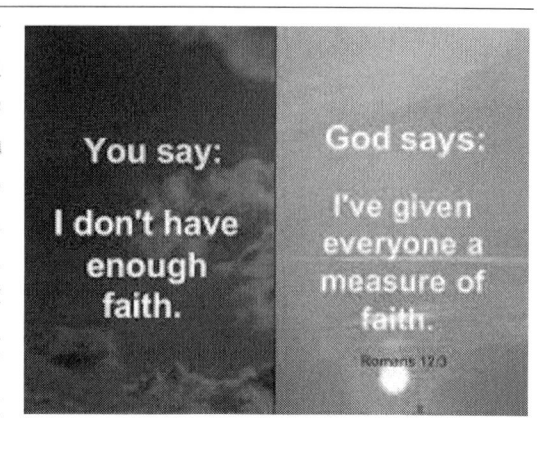

> You say: I don't have enough faith.
>
> God says: I've given everyone a measure of faith.
> Romans 12:3

I was living in sin and I knew it. I wanted to *do my own thing.* To put it quite simply—I was in rebellion. The Bible warns that if we hear His voice we are not to ignore Him...

> **But never forget the warning: "Today you must listen to his voice. Don't harden your hearts against him as Israel did when they rebelled."**
>
> **And who were those people who rebelled against God, even though they heard his voice? Weren't they the ones Moses led out of Egypt?**
>
> **And who made God angry for forty years? Wasn't it the people who sinned, whose bodies fell in the wilderness?**
>
> **And to whom was God speaking when he vowed that they would never enter his place of rest? He was speaking to those who disobeyed him.**
>
> **So we see that they were not allowed to enter his rest because of their unbelief. (Hebrews 3:15-19) NLT**

Like the children of Israel, I found out the hard way what it means to rebel against God and His truth. I had no rest. My rebellion cost me my spiritual life. Yes, I was existing physically, but spiritually I was a walking dead man. When at the age of 16 I decided to return to my sinful ways — <u>life ended up having no real purpose for me, other than trying to find some source for pleasure</u>.

Change is a process, not an event.

That became harder to do, as I went deeper into sin. Life didn't even seem worth living at times. I thought by changing my appearance, or moving to a new place, or by finding new friends, my life would *change*. None of these things changed the reality of my guilt, <u>loneliness and depression</u>. I found out the only way to change my life was to allow God to change my heart, because we cannot change our own hearts.

Jesus Christ is God

This happens only by receiving the light or life of God when we truly believe that Jesus *<u>Christ as God was born in the flesh</u>*. There are many people who profess to believe in God, but do not believe that Jesus Christ *was God* while on earth.

For many deceivers are entered into the world, who confess not that <u>Jesus Christ</u> (as God) <u>is come in the flesh</u>. This is a deceiver and an antichrist. KJV (2 John 7) (Parenthesis mine)

I and my Father are <u>one</u>. (John 10:30) KJV

The word "one" in the above text is the Greek word (Strong's) 1520 ***heis*** (hice) which can mean a number, or to state emphatically that something or someone is "one and same." Thus Jesus said that He was the *same* as His Father ...both were "God."

Because Jesus was God and man, He understands how we as mere humans are powerless against sin that causes us to be separated from God. Therefore, because God the Father loved us so much, He paid the price required by His own law, to set us free from our fallen sinful nature—by providing the way for our pardon and release from sin's eternal death penalty in hell. God's law required that only innocent, *sin free blood*, be shed as payment for our sins.

And almost all things are <u>by (God's) law</u> purged with blood and <u>without the shedding of blood there is no remission</u> (forgiveness and deliverance from sin). KJV (Hebrews 9:22) (Parenthesis mine)

Jesus Christ, who had sinless blood, died on the cross so all humanity could be given the opportunity to experience forgiveness for their sins, by putting their faith in Him as their Lord and Savior.

...the blood of Christ, who through the eternal Spirit offered Himself without spot to God. (Hebrews 9:14) NKJV

For God so loved the world, that he gave his only begotten Son, that whosoever believes in him should not perish, but <u>have everlasting life</u>. (John 3:16) KJV

We cannot be saved from our sin and separation from God and the eternal punishment in hell we so deserve, unless we receive God's gift of eternal light and life by faith in Jesus Christ.

For the wages of sin is death; but <u>the gift of God is eternal life</u> through Jesus Christ <u>our Lord</u>. (Romans 6:23) KJV

When we are willing to believe and *confess with our mouth* that we are receiving Jesus as Savior and <u>Lord</u> of our life… it is at that moment we receive spiritual life from Him!!

That if you shall confess with your mouth the Lord Jesus, and shall believe in your heart that God has raised him from the dead, thou shall be saved.… For with the heart man believes unto righteousness; and <u>with the mouth confession is made unto salvation</u>. (Romans 10:9-10) NKJV

Jesus also said...

Whosoever therefore shall <u>confess me before men</u>, him will I confess also before my Father which is in heaven. But whosoever shall deny me before men, him will <u>I also deny before my Father which is in heaven</u>. (Matthew 10:32-33) KJV

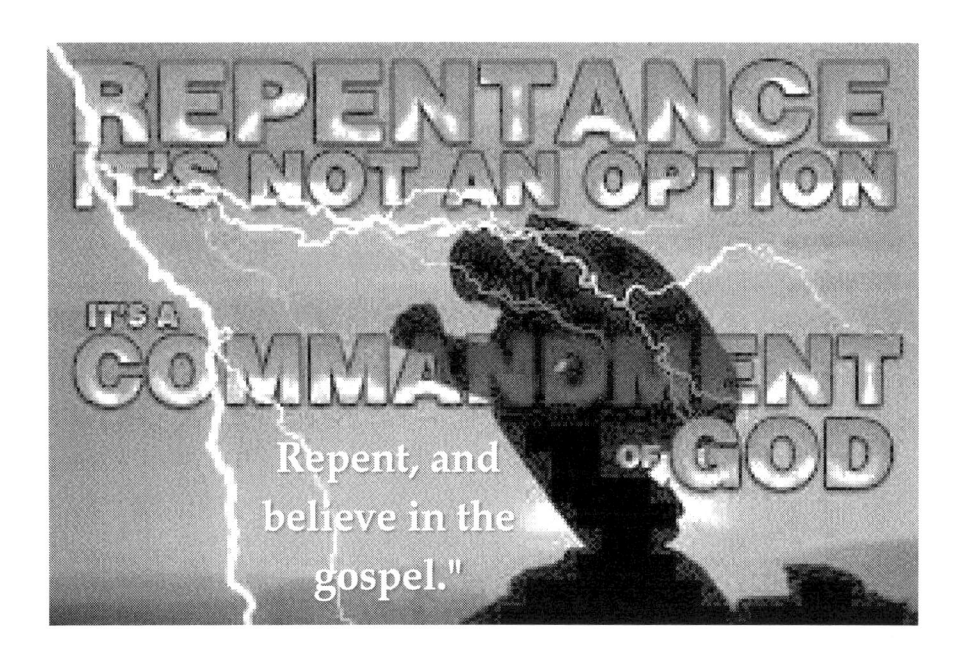

"REPENTANCE IT'S NOT AN OPTION IT'S A COMMANDMENT OF GOD — Repent, and believe in the gospel."

Through changing our mind by repenting of our sin and by our confession of faith in Jesus Christ as Lord and Savior, this causes our spirit to be *born again and receive spiritual life*. At the moment we repent and confess our belief in the gospel message that Jesus came to die for our sins—we pass from death into life. Jesus said...

"**Most assuredly, I say to you, <u>he who hears My word</u>** (the gospel message of salvation) <u>**and believes in Him**</u> (God the Father) **who sent Me, has everlasting life, and shall not come into judgment, but <u>has passed from death into life</u>**. (John 5:24) NKJV

We can go to church, read the Bible, be a good person, or do many good works—but none of these things mean we are born-again and have received eternal life. This only comes by personally <u>believing, receiving and confessing</u> Jesus Christ as our **Lord** and **Savior**.

As I have already mentioned—when we receive the gift of eternal life our name is then recorded in God's <u>Book of Life</u>. Only those who have their names written in the Book of Life will escape eternal torment in hell…

And I saw the dead, small and great, stand before God; and the books were opened: and another book was opened, which is the <u>book of life</u> : and the dead were judged out of those things which were written in the books, <u>according to their works</u>….And the sea gave up the dead which were in it; and death and hell delivered up the dead which were in them: and they were judged every man according to their works...And death and hell were cast into the lake of fire. This is the second death…. And <u>whosoever was not found written in the book of life was cast into the lake of fire</u>. (Revelation 20:12-15) KJV

We are all going to stand before God's judgment seat and give an account of all we have done. Those who did not seek God will be judged for every sin that is recorded in God's books. Only those who are true born-again believers, who have true faith in the cleansing blood of Jesus Christ, will be saved and not be cast into hell for their sins…

For God shall bring every work into judgment, with every secret thing, whether it be good, or whether it be evil. (Eccl 12:14) KJV

...for we shall all stand before the judgment seat of Christ... For it is written, As I live, said the Lord, every knee shall bow to me, and every tongue shall confess to God... So then <u>every one of us shall give account of himself to God</u>. (Romans 14:10-12) KJV

True Faith

Only true faith can save us from God's condemnation. True Faith requires...

#1 We are convinced the Bible is the foundation for all truth.

#2 We are willing to trust and embrace that truth.

#3 We are willing to obey and do what the truth requires.

Not only does God lead, instruct and correct us in this life according to the Bible—we will also be judged according to what is contained in His Word when the 66 books of the Bible are opened when we stand before His judgment throne. All we do and believe must be according to God's standard for truth. This means we must have faith that the Bible itself is the result of men being inspired by God to write what they wrote, so we could find the way to salvation and knowing Him.

<u>All Scripture is inspired by God</u> and is useful <u>to teach us</u> what is true and to make us realize what is wrong in our lives. It <u>straightens us out</u> and teaches us to do what is right.
It is God's way of preparing us in every way, fully equipped for every good thing God wants us to do. (2 Timothy 3:16-17) NLT

More will be said concerning the authenticity and reliability of the Bible in the last chapter of this book. To sum it all up then, there is only one way to find eternal life and to come into a living personal relationship with God the Father.

That way is by accepting Jesus Christ as our Lord and Savior. Through Him we can know for sure that we will live eternally with Him after we die. We must confess with our mouth and tell God we do receive Jesus Christ as our personal Lord and Savior. This is HOW I *got a life* through being born again...

Marvel not that I said unto You, You must be born again. (John 3:3) KJV

We Can Know for Sure That We Are Born again

- Have you ever with your mouth confessed that you believe in your heart Jesus Christ is God the Son—who shed His sinless blood so your sins could be forgiven?
- Have you ever believed in your heart and confessed with your mouth that Jesus died and rose from the dead?

A Prayer of Repentance

Perhaps you have done these things at one point in your life, but like I did, you have also rebelled against God and have turned back to a life of sin and self-gratification, and would now like to come back to God your Father. On the other hand, you may never have confessed these things and would like to be born again. If so, simply read *out loud from your heart* the following prayer (or in your own words say confess these things) ...

Father in Heaven... *With my mouth I am now confessing and believing in my heart that Jesus Christ is God—your Son, who died and shed His blood for me. I also confess and believe in my heart that Jesus rose again from the dead. I now receive Him as my Lord and Savior. I ask Heavenly Father, that you forgive me and cleanse me of all my sins because of my faith in the death and resurrection of Jesus Christ...* [Now confess all sins that come to your mind]. *I ask you Father God to forgive me of these sins. I am willing to turn away from them and I am ready to follow Jesus Christ as Lord of my life, as long as I live. Thank you for your forgiveness and for giving me my new life! Amen*

If you prayed this prayer of repentance—it is important to make sure you tell someone what you just did! Your spirit now has the light and life of God living within in you. Always remember, because you prayed that prayer, and meant it from your heart—God has cleansed you from all your past sin. You are completely and forever forgiven!! He has removed ALL your sins from your heavenly record! Never to be held against you...

As far as the east is from the west, so far has he removed our transgressions from us.
Like as a father pities his children, so the LORD pities them that fear him.
For he knows our frame; he remembers that we are dust. (Psalm 103:12-14) KJV

When we are forgiven, this means we don't have to try to make amends for all our past sins or try to earn God's approval and forgiveness—we have it! We only need to have faith in the blood of Jesus Christ. That causes us to be declared *not guilty* before the judge of the entire universe. We have now been accepted as part of God's beloved family!

If we confess our sins, he is faithful and just to forgive us our sins, and to cleanse us from all unrighteousness. (1 John 1:9) KJV

This how we are <u>continually forgiven</u> of any sins we may fall into after we are born again. It is through our continued faith in the blood of Jesus Christ, that we remain innocent and stay pure and holy in God's sight.

You Have a Glorious Eternal Destiny

Always remember that God loves you and wants to give you everything you need to grow strong in your new faith. Being born again is the first step into your *destined journey* with God. This means God, before you were born, made plans for your life.

Living for God is a daily adventure. It is truly comforting to know He is in control of your life. He is there to make Himself real to you and to help you walk in all He has planned for you.

Listen to what the prophet Isaiah said about his destiny. If you allow Jesus Christ to be the master of your life, you too will find what God has planned for your life.

The LORD called me before my birth; from within the womb he called me by name (Isaiah 49:1) KJV

It is an awesome thought that God knew you before you were ever born! <u>Always remember He has a plan for your life</u>.

For I know the plans I have for you," says the LORD. "They are plans for good and not for disaster, to give you a future and a hope. (Jeremiah 29:11) NLT

This means nothing can or will happen in your life that your heavenly father is not fully aware of. Things may not always go the way you want them to or the way that you think they should go, but always keep in mind that God is always right there and will never leave you!

...for he has said, <u>I will never leave</u> you, nor forsake you. (Hebrews 13:5) NKJV

Learning to hear and obey God's voice and following the leading of His Holy Spirit is crucial—because you have an enemy, called the Satan—the devil. He will try to stop you from following Jesus Christ as the LORD of your life, but only you can determine who will rule—as LORD of your life—will it be Jesus, Satan or you?

And now, just as you accepted Christ Jesus as <u>your Lord</u>, you must continue to live in obedience to him… Let your roots grow down into him and draw up nourishment from him, so you will grow in faith, strong and vigorous in the truth you were taught. Let your lives overflow with thanksgiving for all he has done… Don't let anyone lead you astray… (Colossians 2:6-8) NLT

CHAPTER 2

Counting the Cost

The Bible tells us Moses was a man who understood there was a price to be paid for choosing to allow God to be the LORD of his life—rather than enjoying the pleasures that sin can give us. God can greatly use a person who, like Moses, chooses to follow Him and to pay the price of surrendering their will to God— rather than allowing their will to rule their life.

**24 It was by faith that Moses, when he grew up, refused to be treated as the son of Pharaoh's daughter.
25 He chose to share the oppression of God's people instead of enjoying the fleeting pleasures of sin for a season.
26 He thought it was better to suffer for the sake of the Messiah than to own the treasures of Egypt, for he was looking ahead to the great reward that God would give him. (Hebrews 11:24-26) NLT**

The Bible says there can be pleasure or fun in sin, but only for a *season*. When that season is over—then we must face the consequences for that season of sin. The old saying is very true—*you play—you pay,* because sin always has its consequences:

For the wages of sin is death; but the gift of God is eternal life through Jesus Christ our Lord. (Romans 6:23) KJV

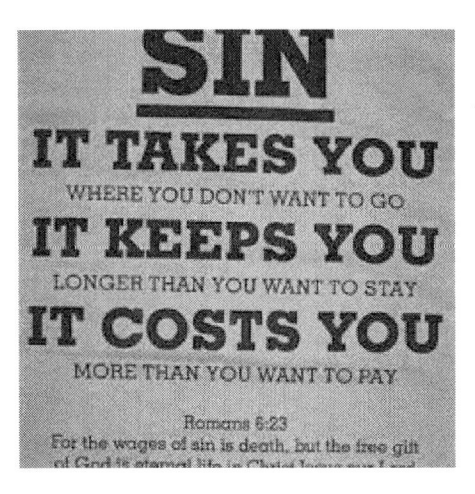

Like Moses, we must choose to follow God even if it isn't always *fun*. I remember hearing someone once say... *"sin will take you where you don't want to go... keep you longer than you want to stay" and cost you more than you want to pay.* On the other hand, God's rewards for our love and faithfulness to Him will take us far beyond what we can even think or imagine… and keep us secure and in peace, if we are willing to pay the price of total self-surrender to God.

That is what the Scriptures mean when they say, "No eye has seen, no ear has heard, and no mind has imagined what God has prepared for those who love him." (1 Corinthians 2:9) NLT

We must receive Jesus as Lord and Savior, for He cannot be our Savior unless He is our Lord. When this is the case—we have become a new creation because we have received a new nature, which no longer desires to sin. We may be tempted to sin and even fall into sin, but we will not want to stay in that sin. After being born again, it wasn't until I made Jesus my LORD —that I lost my taste for the sinful things I once enjoyed—such as partying and drinking, which were a big part of my past immoral lifestyle. Anyone who claims to be a Christian and still has a taste for sin and its pleasures, have not died to the power of sin and have been raised up into their new life in Christ. Because the new life—has God's nature, which hates sin!

I remember just days after being born again, I was celebrating my 21st birthday by being taken to a night club for dinner and a night of drinking. As I sat there with a drink in my hand, I could hardly believe the fact that I really had *no desire* to be in that night club or to drink and party—in fact I couldn't get out of that place fast enough!

For we died and were buried with Christ by (water) **baptism... For when we died with Christ we were set free from the power of sin... In those days, when you were slaves of sin, you weren't concerned with doing what was right. (Rom 6:4, 7, 20) NLT**

> **NO Appetite for Sin ANY LONGER!**

When God's life has been conceived and is growing within us, we lose our appetite for sin. We actually want to do what is right and pure more than we want to give in to our old sin nature (which is still present in us and desires to sin). However, our new born again nature detests what is displeasing to God, and desires to do what is pleasing to Him.

For God is working in you, giving you the desire to obey him and the power to do what pleases him. (Philippians 2:13) NLT

However, this can only happen if we are willing to yield to our new nature and allow it to be what protects us. The Bible says the *new nature* given to us when we are born again—is like a *garment.* If we do not wear the garment of our new Christ-like nature—we will not be walking (living in or wearing) our new born-again nature.

Instead, there must be a spiritual renewal of your thoughts and attitudes.
You must (if you are born-again) **display a new nature because you are a new person, created in God's likeness — righteous, holy, and true.**
So put away all (sin)... (Ephesians 4:23-25) NLT

There are some important things to take into consideration when it comes to making the decision to become a true disciple of Jesus Christ.

1.

The Cost of True Discipleship

There is the price of self-surrender you must pay if Jesus is to be Lord of your life! Our old man or sin nature will still want to do the old sinful things it enjoys, but we must choose to put on our new man or nature.

"Putting on the new man" means making our old nature come "under" subjection or obedience to our new nature. Instead of walking around *naked* and in *shame* (representing our old sin nature) we must put on the new garment—our new nature that desires righteousness—holiness—and truth.

We must make the decision to put <u>on</u> this new garment every day—just as we must get dressed every day so our naked body does not cause us shame. A naked body is also subject to sickness (sin) because it is unprotected from the elements around us.

If we don't clothe ourselves with our new man then only our old man (sin nature) will be manifest (be seen). The more we clothe ourselves with the new—the more we deprive the old nature of its power to influence our life, then our sin nature is made subject to (made to obey) our new born-again nature.

I have heard it said, "You are what you wear," because this how others see you—and in the case of putting on our *new man* or our *new nature* this couldn't be more true!

Don't lie to each other, for you have stripped off your old evil nature and all its wicked deeds... In its place <u>you have clothed yourselves with a brand-new nature</u> that is continually being renewed as you learn more and more about Christ, who created this new nature within you. (Colossians 3:9-10) NLT

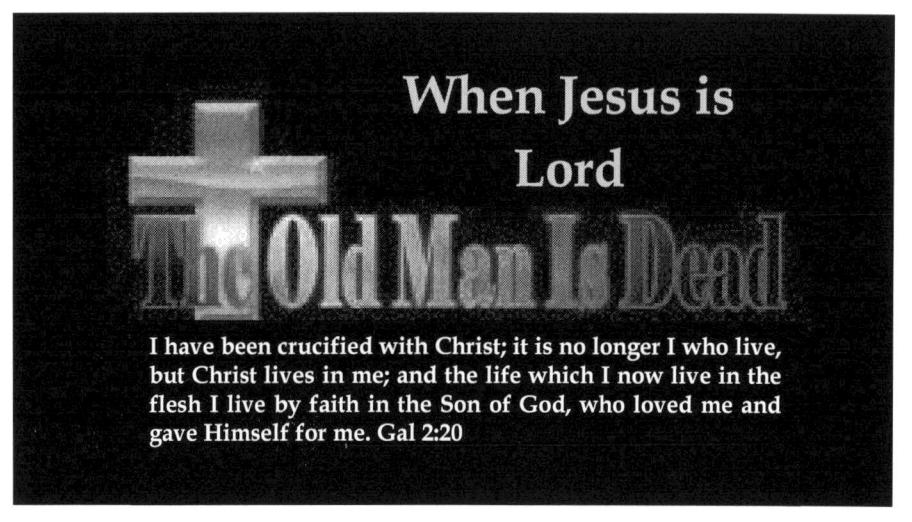

> ### When Jesus is Lord
> ### The Old Man Is Dead
>
> I have been crucified with Christ; it is no longer I who live, but Christ lives in me; and the life which I now live in the flesh I live by faith in the Son of God, who loved me and gave Himself for me. Gal 2:20

<u>When Jesus Christ becomes Lord, we are no longer the masters of our life—Jesus is</u>! If He is not allowed to be our Lord—then we have failed to "put on the new man" and this means the "old man" has not died. It is only when Jesus Christ is truly Lord of our life that He can save (keep us free) from all sin.

This is where I missed the boat when I got "born again" at the age of fourteen. I confessed Jesus as my Savior, but would not make him my Lord by *following* Him as a disciple who obeyed what my new nature was learning in His Word.

Jesus said to the people <u>who believed in him</u>, "You are truly my disciples <u>if you keep obeying my teachings</u>. (John 8:31) NLT

Jesus told those who wanted to follow Him as disciples in this new life—to count the cost if they were going to follow Him.

"But don't begin until you <u>count the cost</u>.... So no one can become my disciple without giving up everything for me. (Luke 14:28, 33) NLT

If we are not willing to give up pet sins, ungodly friendships, personal ambitions, or whatever stands in our way of following Jesus, we have not really decided to make Him the Lord of our life.

So then, since Christ suffered physical pain, you must arm yourselves with the same attitude he had, and be ready to suffer, too. For <u>if you are willing to suffer for Christ, you have decided to stop sinning</u>.
And you won't spend the rest of your life chasing after evil desires, but you will be anxious to do the will of God... You have had enough in the past of the evil things that godless people enjoy--their immorality and lust, their feasting and drunkenness and wild parties, and their terrible worship of idols.
Of course, your former friends are very surprised when you no longer join them in the wicked things they do, and they say evil things about you.
But just remember that they will have to face God, who will judge everyone, both the living and the dead. (1Peter 4:1-4) NLT

Depriving our old sin nature of its desire to sin—is definitely a form of *suffering*. It is a sacrifice we must be willing to make if we are sincerely wanting to be a Christian! Every time we say no to sin we are allowing our sinful nature to be crucified with Christ. I no longer struggle with the old sinful desires I once enjoyed before I became a true Christian. They have been nailed to the cross and have lost their power over my life! This doesn't mean I never sin—when I do I simply become honest and confess my sin and bring it to the cross of Jesus Christ. This is how sin loses its power in our lives.

Our old sinful selves were crucified with Christ so that sin might lose its power in our lives. We are no longer slaves to sin. (Romans 6:6) NLT

Our sinful human nature gets crucified every time we confess our sins. What a joy to know we don't have to live in condemnation and guilt, but can simply be honest with God and receive forgiveness every time we confess our sins!

If we confess our sins, he is faithful and just to forgive us our sins, and to cleanse us from all unrighteousness. (1 John 1:9) KJV

If we have really made Jesus our Lord and Savior, we will not willingly sin. Which means we will not willing continue on in anything we know is sinful. The shed blood of Jesus Christ on that horrible cross is the place of sacrifice that paid the price for the remission or forgiveness of our sin. Without the cross of Jesus where would we be?

For if we sin willfully after that we have received the knowledge of the truth, there remains no more sacrifice for sins.

But a certain fearful looking for of judgment and fiery indignation, which shall devour the adversaries. (Heb 10:26-27) KJV

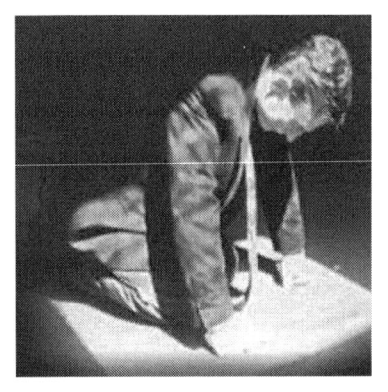

Wilful sin is sin we are not willing to turn away from (repent of). The blood of Jesus cannot cleanse sin we are not willing to confess and turn away from. The Bible is clear that we must be willing to repent which means change our mind and turn away from all sin...

...that they should repent and turn to God, and do works meet for repentance. (Acts 26:20) KJV

True repentance doesn't just mean we are willing to admit we have sinned or that we are willing to say we are sorry. God is not simply looking for an apology when we sin. He is looking for the *fruit of repentance.*

Bring forth fruit that is consistent with repentance—let your lives prove your change of heart. (Matthew 3:8) AMP

True repentance means we have been *converted*. We come into agreement with God concerning our sin. We no longer justify it, blame it on someone or something else, or ignore it. But we become honest by *confessing it* and *turning from it*.

<u>Repent</u> ...and <u>be converted</u>, that your sins may be blotted out, when the times of refreshing shall come from the presence of the Lord. (Acts 3:19) KJV

As I have said, we will always have to face being tempted to sin. However, God promises to help us in those times...

But remember that the temptations that come into your life are no different from what others experience. And God is faithful. He will keep the temptation from becoming so strong that you can't stand up against it. When you are tempted, <u>he will show you a way out</u> so that you will not give in to it. (1 Corinthians 10:13) NLT

2.

The Rewards of Discipleship

The Lord rewards true disciples by giving them a way out of the temptation to sin. The way out of temptation is <u>not</u> just by using our <u>sheer will power</u>. We on our own do not have the power to overcome sin. On the other hand, <u>if we have the will—He has the power</u>. Jesus promised His disciples (then and now) they would receive the all power they needed...

But you shall receive power, after the Holy Spirit has come upon you. (Act 1:8) NKJV

We are all infected and impure with sin. When we proudly display our righteous deeds, we find they are but filthy rags. (Isaiah 64:6) NLT

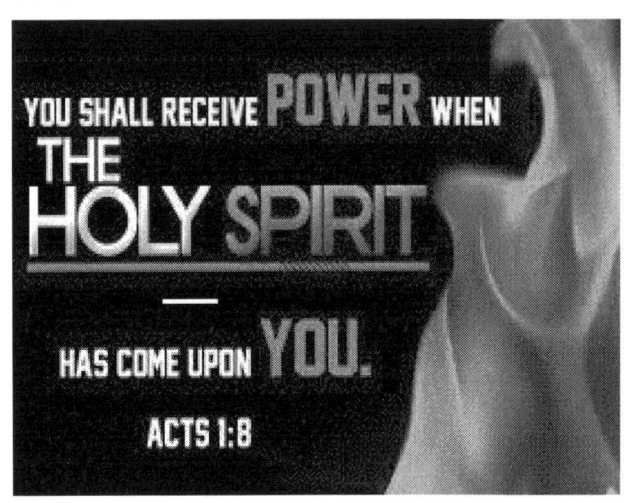

When we try to make our self-right with God apart from the blood of Jesus, our pride is telling God, "I don't believe confessing my sin and putting my faith in the blood of Jesus... is enough, I'll do "right" things to make myself right with you!" God wants us to put our faith in the blood of Jesus and power of His Holy Spirit—to become right and live right. He does not want us to place our confidence in our *will power* or *self-sufficiency* to be right and live right for Him. Therefore, without the power of the Holy Spirit we will strive to live for God and do what He has called us to do through our own power, which causes pride to rule our life. It is very humbling to know and admit we need God's help.

This is the word of the LORD... saying, not by (your) **might, nor by** (your) **power, but by my spirit, says the LORD of hosts. (Zechariah 4:6) KJV** (Parenthesis mine)

In Chapter Three I will discuss how to receive the power of the Holy Spirit—by being baptized in the Holy Spirit. When we make the decision to become a disciple of Jesus Christ, this means we receive our assignment to operate in the supernatural power of God. In the following verses the last recorded words spoken by Jesus to His disciples are given, which was right before He ascended into heaven. Here are some of the *rewards* He promised to all who would become His faithful disciples ...

And these signs <u>shall</u> follow them that believe; in my name <u>they shall</u> cast out devils; <u>they shall</u> speak with new tongues;

<u>They shall</u> take up serpents; and if they drink any deadly thing, it shall not hurt them; <u>they shall</u> lay hands on the sick, and <u>they shall</u> recover. (Mark 16:17-18) KJV

As a true follower of Jesus Christ we have the power of the Holy Spirit working in us so we can help others get free from their sin, sickness and demons. Another great reward of being a true disciple of Jesus is that His disciples will hear God speak to them.

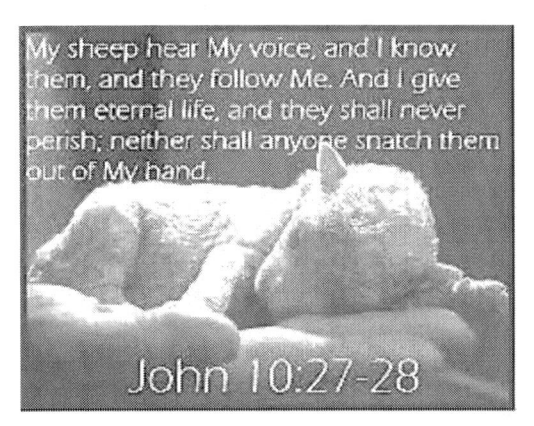

My sheep hear my voice, and I know them, and <u>they follow me</u>...And I give unto them eternal life; and they shall never perish; neither shall any man pluck them out of my hand. (John 10:27-28) KJV

Being able to hear the voice of God is what establishes our personal relationship with Him. If a wife was never to have her husband speak to her—there would be no personal relationship between them. So it is with our relationship with God. God's voice is the Holy Spirit of Jesus speaking to our new born again human spirit.

But the Comforter, which is the Holy Ghost, whom the Father will send in my name, he shall teach you all things... (John 14:26) KJV

His Holy Spirit will guide us, teach us and comfort us when we need answers or are facing temptations, problems or trials. Hearing God speak to us through the Scriptures means we have His presence in our life, which is essential for remaining strong when our faith is being tested.

For when your faith is tested, your endurance has a chance to grow… So let it grow, for when your endurance is fully, developed you will be strong in character and ready for anything. (James 1:3-4) NLT

If we are willing to pay the price of becoming a true follower (disciple) of Jesus Christ it will then be possible to live a life that is free from sin and the guilt it produces. This means we, through the power of God's Holy Spirit, can MORE than conquer any problem, sin or obstacle that would try to keep us from following the way— the truth—the life, which is found in Jesus Christ!

No, in all these things we are <u>more than conquerors</u> through him that loved us. (Romans 8:37) KJV

We Are Justified

One of the greatest rewards of being a true disciple of Jesus Christ is that we can know beyond a shadow of a doubt that God has JUSTIFED us. This means we come before God cleansed of all sin because He looks at us and sees our faith in the blood of Jesus—and we are declared NOT GUILTY in His eyes!

If we feel accused by Satan, when he tries to condemn us for our failures—God tells him <u>we are innocent</u> because we have repented of all sin and we are cleansed by the blood of Jesus Christ. This means it is *just-if-I'd* never sinned! *What a glorious and wonderful reward!*

True disciples *will* live a life that is FREE from sin and the condemnation that it brings into our life. There is no longer any need to fear being rejected by God.

So now <u>there is no condemnation for those who belong to Christ Jesus</u>...For the power of the life-giving Spirit has freed you through Christ Jesus from the power of sin that leads to death. (Romans 8:1-2) NLT

Quenching God's Holy Spirit

We must continually be growing in our faith and love for God through our relationship with Jesus Christ. Otherwise, we may turn back to our old life of sin and again become separated from God. True disciples will find that the rewards for serving God far outweigh the pleasures of sin. We must never forget that when we don't repent of our sin, <u>it will lead to our spiritual death</u>. <u>Never loose sight of the fact that it is possible to die spiritually after being born- again</u>. Once our candle (spirit) receives the light and life of God, it can go out if we choose to *quench the Holy Spirit* by putting Him out of our life through wilful sin—as we have already discussed. **Quench not the Spirit. (1 Thessalonians 5:19) KJV**

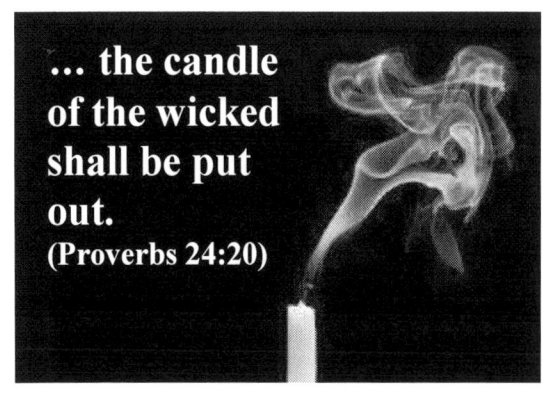

Those who choose to live wickedly in their sin will lose the light of God's light and life upon their spirit (candle).

For there shall be no reward to the evil man; the candle of the wicked shall be put out. (Proverbs 24:20) KJV

Our prayer should be that of King David—who was called a man after God's own heart because despite his failure and sins of adultery and murder, he desired to have a right heart and life with God. David knew the painful consequences of sin and his need for God's forgiveness and restoration…

Create in me a clean heart, O God. Renew a right spirit within me...
Do not banish me from your presence, and don't take your Holy Spirit from me.
Restore to me again the joy of your salvation, and make me willing to obey you.
Then I will teach your ways to sinners, and they will return to you. (Ps 51:10-13) NLT

It is only when we have experienced the wonderful joy of being born again by having our sins cleansed—that we will have the desire to teach other sinners the way to repentance and to experiencing a true and living relationship with God—who loves them. There is no greater joy than to lead another person to Jesus Christ so they can receive the gift of eternal life from God.

The Lord... is not willing that any should perish but that all should come to repentance. (2 Peter 3:9) NKJV

CHAPTER 3

Growing in the New Life

As long as we keep following Jesus Christ by allowing Him to be Lord and Savior over our lives, old sin habits, thoughts and behaviors will die. All of the old addictions, compulsive and bad behaviors didn't die instantly in my life after I was born-again. It has taken and <u>continues to take</u>, the cleansing work of God's Holy Spirit to cause all things to become new. The Bible calls this cleansing work the *sanctifying power* of Holy Spirit…

23 And the very God of peace <u>sanctify you wholly</u> and I pray God your whole spirit and soul and body be preserved blameless unto the coming of our Lord Jesus Christ.

24 Faithful is he that calls you, who also will do it. (1Thessalonians 5:23-24) KJV

More will be explained about God's sanctifying power shortly. However, once we are born-again and have received new life, there must be continued growth (through being sanctified). Just like when a baby is born, it must develop properly in order to fulfil its destiny as an adult. God does not intend for us to remain spiritual babies.

As newborn babes, desire the sincere milk of the word that you may grow thereby. (1 Peter 2:2) KJV

New believers must grow by feeding upon God's Word. After I was born again and made the commitment to follow Jesus as Lord, I wanted to know all I could about God and His plan for my life.

I suggest new believers read the book of Psalms and the Gospel of John to start with, if they are just becoming students of the Bible. New born babies must eat often. They may not eat much at first, but they must eat! If babies are not hungry—something is wrong. Sins are like germs that make us sick. When we are sick we lose our appetite.

Not confessing and turning away from sin makes us spiritually sick and steals our appetite or our desire to study the Word of God. Also, if babies are healthy they will grow and at some point they will get beyond just drinking milk.

At first babies need help and need to be fed by others. In the same way new believers also need help learning how to read and study the word, but eventually they, like natural babies, must grow and learn how to feed themselves.

Growth requires disciplining ourselves to read and study the Bible. It is our spiritual food. It tells us what God desires for us and the kind of character he wants to develop in us. Immature Christians are like babies, because they allow their old nature to rule their lives. If they are not filling themselves with the word of God, they never grow up to be mature or healthy Christians. Paul was telling this to a group of born-again people in his day...

I had to feed you with milk and not with solid food, because you couldn't handle anything stronger. And you still aren't ready,

for you are still controlled by your own sinful desires. You are jealous of one another and quarrel with each other. Doesn't that prove you are controlled by your own desires? You are acting like people who don't belong to the Lord. (1 Corinthians 3:2-3) NLT

Immature Christians, like children, are very *self-centred*. As we mature in Christ, our mind is on how God can use us to help others, rather than on what God can do for us. One reason Christians often struggle with their old sinful fleshly nature, is because they feed their flesh and not their spirit. They spend more time watching TV, listening to secular music, or talk shows (that fill their minds and hearts with the worlds garbage), than they do spending time with God—by studying their Bible and praying.

There are many things that cry out for our attention. Just as our children must be trained to become disciplined, our mind must be trained and disciplined to keep focused upon God's word and on His ways…

Set your affection on things above, not on things on the earth. For you are dead [to your old life], and your [new] life is hid with Christ in God. (Colossians 3:2-3) KJV
The only way we are going to see God change our life, is if we let Him renew our mind through studying His word and finding out what the will of God is in all things.

Don't copy the behavior and customs of this world, but let God transform you into a new person by changing the way you think. Then you will know what God wants you to do and you will know how good and pleasing and perfect his will really is. (Romans 12:2) NLT

The battle is bending and bowing to God's will and not our will— this battle is fought in our mind. Believe me Satan, knows if he can get us to agree with how he thinks, he can control our feelings and our actions. Always remember this—thoughts produce "feelings" and we normally act upon our feelings. The Bible says...

For as (a man) thinks in his heart, so is he... (Proverbs 23:7) KJV (Parenthesis mine)

What we think or choose to believe will determine what kind of a person we will become. If we think we are stupid… we will act stupid—if we think we are no good...we will not do good things. We must therefore, let God and His word change how we think.

Let's examine some of the things the Bible tells us about that are vital to our spiritual life—so we can become all God has destined for us to be.

1. You Must Be Water Baptized

After we have repented of our sins and have made the decision to become a disciple of Jesus Christ, we then need to be water baptized. There is an instance in the book of Acts where some new believers in Jesus Christ had been baptized with the Holy Spirit and had received spiritual gifts, but had not yet been baptized in water, because they did not know about water baptism. No doubt they had been baptized in water by John the Baptist for their repentance for sin, but they had not been baptized in water in Jesus name.

For they heard them speak with tongues and magnify God. Then Peter answered... "Can anyone forbid water, that these should not be baptized who have received the Holy Spirit just as we have?" And he commanded them to be baptized <u>in the name of the Lord</u>. (Acts 10:46-48) NKJV

To be baptized in the "name of Jesus" means we are dying to our old self life and immersing ourselves in the NAME of Jesus. The word *name* in both Hebrew and Greek refers to a person's **character** (nature) and **authority**. This means we are to be **clothed with** the **character** (nature) and **authority** of Jesus Christ. Being baptized in the *name* of Jesus gives us the *authority* to walk in "newness of life"—or the true abundant life that Jesus died to give us.

And that you put on the new man, which after God is created in righteousness and true holiness. (Eph 4:24) NKJV

Jesus said, that if any man wants to be born again, he needs to be **born** (brought forth into the new life) by **water** and by the **Spirit**. Jesus didn't talk about repeating a sinner's prayer; but he did preach repentance towards God.

"The time is fulfilled, and the kingdom of God is at hand. Repent, and believe in the gospel." (Mark 1:15) NKJV

The gospel is the good news about receiving a "new birth" that brings us a new life through Jesus Christ. This new life comes by *doing three things* that requires our faith. The Bible says once we believe the truth about Jesus, we must prove our faith by our works of obedience.

For as the body without the spirit is dead, so faith without works is dead also. (James 2:26) NKJV

FIRST WORK... the true gospel message requires that we must be willing to repent (i.e. change our mind about our sin and be willing to leave it all behind). Repentance is the "proof" that a person is truly believing and agreeing with the gospel message that says sin is our problem.

Therefore, bear fruits worthy of (or corresponding to) **repentance. (Matthew 3:8) NKJV**

True repentance will produce fruit (proof) that we have really changed our mind about sin. One such "proof" will be obedience. We will choose to obey God's Word.

SECOND WORK... our obedience to God requires dying to sin by being buried (baptized) in water—which brings death to our old life of sin so we can be raised up into our new born again life as a true disciple of Jesus Christ.

Many professing Christians may have truly repented of their old life of sin but were not *immediately* and *obediently* baptized in water—as Jesus and the disciples taught. This is because very few today preach this as being necessary to being born again.

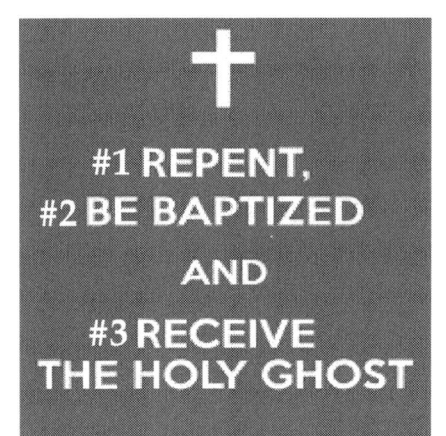

Baptism after repentance is not an option to being born again. To be born again is to be brought forth into newness of life through Jesus Christ. Many think that as long as they tell God they are sorry for their sins and ask Jesus into their heart—they are born again. That is NOT what Jesus and the apostles taught!

It is Biblical to conclude that we are NOT born again until these steps of obedience are taken! Again, Jesus said we are born again (brought forth into a new life) only by WATER and the SPIRIT:

Jesus answered, I say unto you, except a man be born (literally: be brought forth) **by water and by the Spirit, he cannot enter into the kingdom of God. (John 3:5) NKJV** (Parenthesis for clarity).

Baptism is not just a symbolic act: we must take LITERALLY what God's Word is saying about water baptism. Without baptism as an act of obedient faith—there is no death to the power of sin in our life...

Or do you not know that as many of us as were (water) **baptized into Christ Jesus were baptized into His death? ...Therefore we were buried with Him through** (water) **baptism into death, that just as Christ was raised from the dead by the glory of the Father, even so we also** should **walk** (live) **in newness of life... For he who has died has been freed from sin. (Romans 6:3-4, 7) NKJV** (Parenthesis Mine for clarity—the word in gray was inserted by the translators).

Many who claim to be born again may repent of their sin and even get baptized in water—but their baptism was not an act of faith. It is only when we rightly understand, from God's Word, why we are doing something, that it becomes an act of faith. The Bible says: *"faith comes by hearing"* (understanding) (Romans 10:17). It is only when we understand what water baptism is intended to accomplish in us, that we can be baptized in faith.

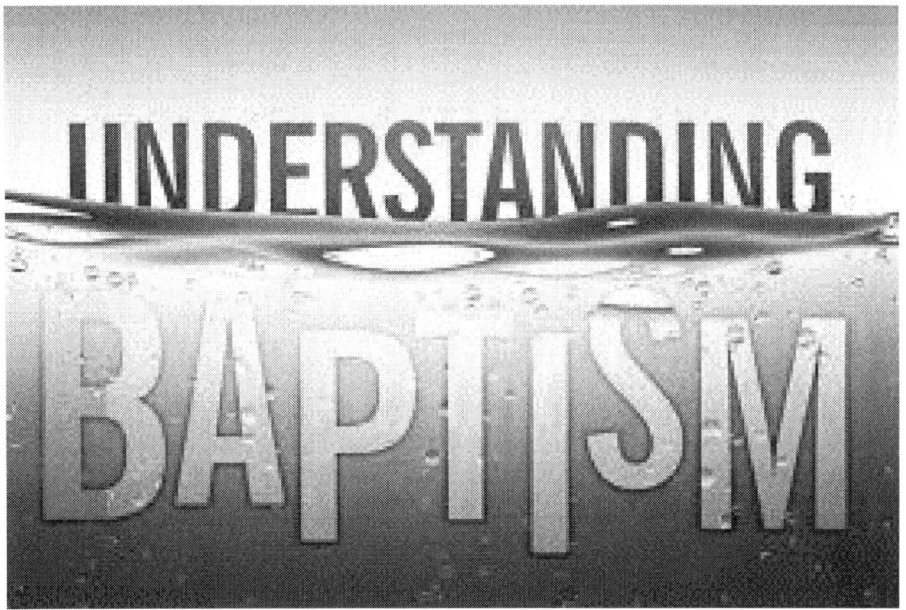

When baptism is not an obedient act of faith—according to *right Biblical doctrine*, it is just another *form of godliness* "religious act" that has no power or effect in our life. Everything we do must be the result of faith that comes by hearing God's Word (Rom 10:17).

Thus, failure to be baptized as an act of <u>obedient faith</u> keeps us slaves to the power of sin. Paul goes on to say the following in his discussion on being baptized into a death that results in a life that is set free from sin ...

But thanks be to God that, though you used to be slaves to sin, you wholeheartedly obeyed the form of doctrine (about water baptism) to which you were entrusted... And (as a result) having been set free from sin, you became slaves of righteousness. (Romans 6:17-18) NKJV (Parenthesis for more literal clarity).

This verse is clear that water baptism—as an obedient act of faith in the doctrine of water baptism, frees us from the power of sin, which allows us to experience "newness of life"—that is the result of being "born again" (brought forth anew) by water and by the spirit.

There are many who think they have been born again, because they have asked for their sins to be forgiven and have asked Jesus to be their Savior, but have not obeyed the *form of doctrine* (about water baptism)—thus they do not walk in "newness of life" as a "professing Christian."

They still struggle with their old sin nature, habits and ways. This is because they have never put to death the power of sin in their life by having obedient faith in water baptism. They are still immersed in their old sin life. Baptism brings death to the power of sin in our life:

Therefore, we were buried with Him through baptism into death, that just as Christ was raised from the dead by the glory of the Father, even so we also should walk in newness of life. For when we died with Christ (by water baptism) **we were set free from the power of sin... So we now consider ourselves dead to sin and able to live for the glory of God through Christ Jesus... now we are free from the power of sin and have become slaves of God. Now we do those things that lead to holiness and result in eternal life. (Romans 6:4, 7, 11, 22) NKJV**

Remember: when we are baptized in water it must be done "in the name of Jesus our Lord." Why? As stated, to be baptized in the "name of Jesus" means we are dying to our old self life and immersing ourselves in the NAME of Jesus. Again, the word *name* in both Hebrew and Greek refers to a person's **character** (nature) and **authority**. This means we are to be **clothed with** the **character** (nature) and **authority** of Jesus Christ. Being baptized in the *name* of Jesus gives us the *authority* to walk in "newness of life"—or the true abundant life that Jesus died to give us.

If we want the power of sin from our old life to die...we must be baptized—then we WILL walk in newness of life. This does not happen without the **power** of God's Holy Spirit. Those who try to live the Christian life without truly being born again—as laid out in the Scriptures—will only have a "form of godliness" because they have **no power** for God's Holy Spirit is not dwelling in them:

" ...Having a <u>form of godliness,</u> (counterfeit Christianity) but <u>denying the power</u> thereof..." (2 Timothy 3:5) NKJV

As a Christian counselor, I find that many who call themselves a "Christian" have not entered into "Christianity" the way Jesus and the apostles taught.

This is also why many professing Christians fall prey to a *counterfeit Christianity* and come under the influence of demonic legalistic religious spirits that demand we strive through human effort or some sort of works to become righteous and to live righteously.

Righteousness is obtained only by entering the Kingdom of God through the new birth, the way that Jesus and His apostles taught! [1] Many also falsely teach or think they can only be baptized by a professional "minister" or that it must be done in a "church." However, the *Bible* is clear that any truly born again believer is a "priest" (minister) unto God, possessing the right and privilege (as a servant of Christ) to obey Jesus by baptizing anyone who has truly repented and desires to follow Jesus Christ as a disciple. **...To Him who loved us and washed us from our sins in His own blood...and has made us kings and priests to His God and Father... (Rev 1:5-6) NKJV.** We only need a bathtub, pool, or lake to baptize and immerse a person in water:

---

[1] Baptism was universally seen by early Christians as necessary for salvation, until Huldrych Zwingli in the 16th century denied its necessity. Elizabeth A. Livingstone (2005). "Baptism". *The Oxford Dictionary of the Christian Church*. Oxford: Oxford University Press. pp. 151–154. ISBN 0-19-280290-9. OCLC 58998735

...the eunuch said, "Look! There's some water! Why can't I be baptized?" (Acts 8:36) NLT

Then Peter said to them, "Repent, and let every one of you be baptized in the name of Jesus Christ for the remission (deliverance) of sins; <u>and you shall receive the gift of the Holy Spirit</u>. (Acts 2:38) NJKV

<u>THIRD WORK</u>... when we have done the "first TWO works" (of repentance and water baptism) ... then, we are to receive the baptism of the Holy Spirit (more will be explained on being baptized with the Holy Spirit later in this chapter). The Holy Spirit is our regenerating (restoring) and renewing (transforming) power. He restores us from sin by revealing to us the Word of God. His revelation of truth transforms our lives by continually delivering us from all known and unknown sin.

God's grace (i.e. which includes God's gifts) are released into our lives through the baptism of the Holy Spirit, without which there is no POWER to walk or live in the "newness of life." This *newness of life* proves the new birth has taken place in us.

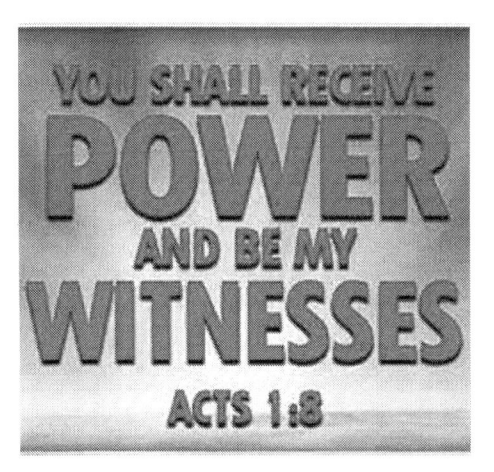

Those who lack the POWER that comes from the Holy Spirit baptism, end up having lives that *contradict God's truth, character and authority.* Those who lack God's truth, character and His power, only have, as mentioned previously, a form of godliness and a *religion* that they follow, because they are not genuinely born again.

Such people claim they know God, but they <u>deny</u> (literally meaning: "<u>contradict</u>") **him by the way they live. (Titus 1:16) NLT**

"... He saved us, through the <u>washing</u> (*water baptism is mentioned first...then), **by <u>regeneration</u> and <u>renewing</u> by the Holy Spirit... whom He poured out on us abundantly through** (our faith in) **Jesus Christ our Savior..." (Titus 3:5-6) NJKV** (Parenthesis mine for clarity).

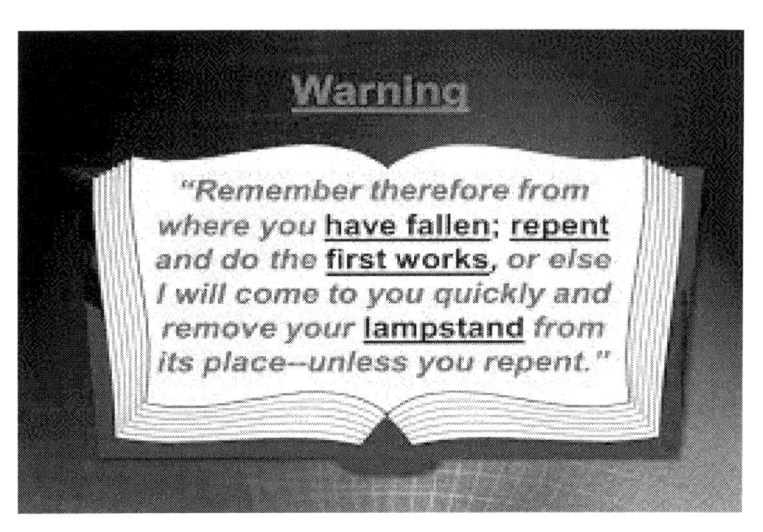

> **Warning**
>
> "Remember therefore from where you **have fallen**; **repent** and do the **first works**, or else I will come to you quickly and remove your **lampstand** from its place—unless you repent."

When Christians Backslide

Many times when a professing Christian "backslides into sin" and they truly come back again to God and repent, they fail to realize that they need to do their first works over again as Jesus taught:

Remember then from where you have fallen (or backslidden); **repent and <u>do the first works</u>** (be baptized in water and with the Holy Spirit) **or else I will come to you quickly and remove your lampstand from its place — unless you repent. (Rev 2:5)** (Parenthesis Mine for clarity).

When I repented of my sin and confessed Jesus Christ as my savior at age 14, I failed to be baptized in water and with the Holy Spirit. As a result, I eventually became a backslider and like a prodigal child, I lived in great sin. When I repented and came back to the Lord at the age of 21, this time I was baptized in water and with the Holy Spirit. This has enabled me to be truly converted (truly transformed) and to "walk in newness of life" since that time.

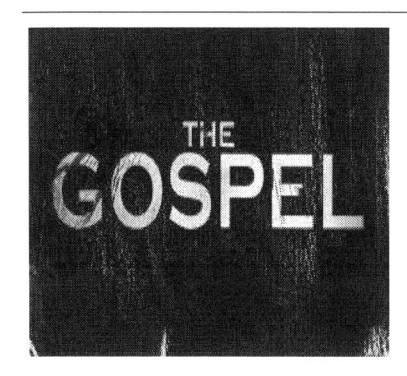

A backslider has quenched God's light (or life from their spirit) and their spirit (candle) needs to be relit (regenerated) to bring forth (God's life or light) again (this was discussed on pgs. 15-16). Without doing the first works of repentance and baptism for *re-birth* the backslider will not experience deliverance from the power of sin by God's Spirit.

When we do not follow <u>exactly</u> **the way**, which Jesus and the apostles taught, on how to enter the Kingdom of God, which is by being born again —we cannot enter the Kingdom of God, until we do it as they taught.

For the kingdom of God is... righteousness, and peace, and joy in the Holy Ghost. (Romans 14:17) NJKV

"...For indeed, the kingdom of God is within you." (Luke 17:21) NJKV

... Jesus answered, "Most assuredly, I say to you, unless one is born again, he cannot see the kingdom of God... unless one is born of water and the Spirit, he cannot enter the kingdom of God. (John 3:3, 5) NJKV

In fact, far too many think they are born again because they may of had a very emotional (soulish experience) when they asked Jesus into their heart and sincerely promised to follow Him for the rest of their life.

They may have even cried out and asked God to forgive their sins and to "save" them, but unless they have obediently followed what Jesus taught as the only way to receive salvation (deliverance) from sin... they cannot be saved (delivered) from the power of sin. Only those who endure to the end by remaining free from sin, will be saved from hell in the end. **Many have had their "past sins" forgiven when they asked God for forgiveness because of their faith in the blood of Christ, but do not go on to walk in <u>newness of life</u> where the power of sin is broken over their lives. Therefore, the power of sin still rules their lives.**

But he who endures to the end shall be saved. (Matthew 24:13) NKJV

The Apostol Paul had to deal with people who called them Christians but still lived in sin. The Bible talks about people who are "false Christians" who we are told not to allow in our churches or to fellowship with. The Apostle Paul had to deal with a group of people like this and this is what he said:

For I am afraid that when I come I won't like what I find, and you won't like my response. I am afraid that I will find quarreling, jealousy, anger, selfishness, slander, gossip, arrogance, and disorderly behavior... Yes, I am afraid that when I come again, God will humble (dishonor) me in your presence. And I will be grieved because many of you have not given up your old sins. You have not repented of your impurity, sexual immorality, and eagerness for lustful pleasure... This is the third time I am coming to visit you and as the Scriptures say, "The facts of every case must be established by the testimony of two or three witnesses"... I have already warned those who had been sinning when I was there on my second visit. Now I again warn them and all others, just as I did before, that next time I will not spare them...Examine yourselves to see if your faith is genuine. (2 Cor 12:19-13:2, 5) NLT

Now we command you, brothers, in the name of our Lord Jesus Christ, that you withdraw yourselves from every brother who walks in rebellion, and not after the tradition which they received from us. (2 Thessalonians 3:6) World English Bible

...because of some so-called Christians there—false ones, really—... we refused to give in to them for a single moment. (Gal 2:4-5) NLT

Let me say however, God will always hear the person who sincerely cries out to Him for salvation. This is when the mercy and goodness of God will eventually draw that person to the truth, of the gospel so they can understand their need for true repentance, and baptism by water and being baptized with the Holy Spirit. These are the means for keeping sin out of our life **"...the goodness of God leads you to repentance." (Romans 2:4)**

Again, this comes only by hearing the true gospel when it is given to them. Jesus said, **"...no one can come to Me unless the Father who sent Me draws him..." (John 6:44)**

No matter how you cut it, it isn't until people actually HEAR (understand) the true gospel message about who Jesus is, and what He came to do, that they can believe the truth (true gospel) regarding how to enter the Kingdom of God.

Because of not hearing the true gospel message, multitudes sit in churches with false ideas about who Jesus is—and why He died. They don't hear how to become a true follower of Jesus. This is because another gospel about another Jesus is being brought forth by a deceiving spirit which is laying a false foundation for their faith.

For "Anyone who calls on the name of the Lord will be saved." ...But how can they call on him to save them unless they believe in (the true gospel about) him? And how can they believe in him if they have never heard (the true gospel about) **about him? And how can they hear about him unless someone tells them (the truth)? (Romans 10:13-14)** NLT (Parenthesis mine for clarity).

When a person's "Christianity" is the result of not responding to the TRUE GOSPEL message—those in this place go on to believe a false gospel (such as the very popular self-enhancement gospel, a gnostic gospel or the false prosperity gospel). A false gospel leads to following another Jesus—

> **The true gospel is a call to self-denial. It is not a call to self-fulfillment.**

one that has been created from the mind of man and not according to the Bible. Responding to a false gospel that gives us a false idea about who Jesus is, leads people into being deceived and led by lying religious and seducing spirits that are more than able to give them false teachings, counterfeit gifts and demonic supernatural experiences to foster their deception.

You seem to believe whatever anyone tells you, even if they preach about a <u>different Jesus</u> than the one we preach, or a <u>different Spirit</u> than the one you received, or a <u>different kind of gospel</u> than the one you believed—from us. (2 Cor 11:4) NLT

If we do not follow what Jesus taught, and think we can enter the kingdom of God *some other way* than what is plainly laid out in Scripture… we are deceived and will also lead others into experiencing a false conversion that robs them of the only "WAY" into the kingdom.

Jesus, called Himself the "door" through which we must enter. This means we cannot experience being born again nor enter into the Kingdom of God, unless it is done <u>His way</u>. **Jesus is the way, the truth and the life (Jn 14:6)**. Obedience to His way is the only way to enter His sheepfold.

Verily, verily, I say unto you, He that enters not by the door into the sheepfold, but climbs up <u>some other way</u>, the same is a thief and a robber. (John 10:1)

God calls us a *thief* when we take upon ourselves the name of "Christian" and have entered Christianity some other way.

Keep in mind that Jesus, at the time He lived on earth, could not baptize anyone with the Holy Spirit or with water, because the old covenant had not yet been replaced with the new covenant which came into being by His death.

After the cross we see the fulfillment of the new birth Jesus was talking about in (John 3:5). It is after the cross we see Peter standing up and saying, **"Repent, and let every one of you be baptized in the name of Jesus Christ for the remission of (deliverance from) sins; and then you shall receive the gift of the Holy Spirit." (Acts 2:38)**

The Abundant life is Doing What Jesus Did!

True Christians want more than just living a life of where they get up every morning to go to work, come home, eat dinner, veg out for hours in front of the boob tube or go surfing on the net until they go to bed – only to start all over again the next day.

They may even attend a mid-week Bible study, be involved in many "church programs," read and listen to multitudes of Christian materials—yet as useful as these may be, all this is not the abundant life Jesus died to give us.

The true abundant life comes only by doing what Jesus commanded His disciples to do—which is to be *doing the work of the ministry* by making disciples through leading people to repentance from sin and praying for people to be healed and set free of demons! There has been a true remnant of Christians in every generation just as there is a last day's remnant now who are not afraid to give up everything to follow Jesus! Do you see yourself training, equipping and making discipeling of others?

Can you see yourself bringing life to the body of Christ? As Torben Sondergaard teaches: "The modern church is facing a real crisis. A crisis that goes deeper than any previous need for reformation. A crisis brought about by hundreds of years of church traditions, suffocating structures and countless meetings in church buildings that have failed to produce productive disciples of Jesus Christ.

True disciples of Jesus in these end times are beginning to experience a yearning to get back to what we read in the Book Acts: A simple, true disciple-life style that is led by the Holy Spirit, where the kingdom of God comes near in homes, on the streets, in shops – yes, all places where people are."

How many professing Christians see themselves working full time for the Lord... bringing sinners to repentance and into the kingdom of God—for the rest of their life? Christians who are awakened to these truths as true disciples of Jesus, they will be making disciples.

Those who are passionate about Jesus will truly hunger to live as disciples of Jesus—as is demonstrated in the Book of Acts. How many Christian leaders are truly making new disciples of Jesus and training them to do the TRUE work of the ministry Jesus gave to us?

> He (Jesus) is the one who gave these gifts to the church: the apostles, the prophets, the evangelists, and the pastors and teachers... Their responsibility is to equip God's people to do his work and build up the church, the body of Christ. (Eph 4:11-12) NLT

The work of the ministry for genuine Christian leaders is that of teaching others by example, how to lead people to repentance and to being born again and how to pray for people to be healed, set free of demons and to be baptized with the Holy Spirit. Far too many church leaders are busy making their own followers, rather than followers of Jesus. These kinds of leaders require salaries and a tax exempt status—they are nothing more than "hirelings." A true leader leads like our Good Shepherd Jesus. **The hireling runs away** (when he is threatened) **because he is merely hired and has no real concern for the sheep. (John 10:13)**

There are so many "religious" works happening in churches, that are being called the "work of the ministry"—but is it really the work of the ministry as Jesus defined it? We as Christians are ALL going to stand before Christ and be held accountable for whether or not we brought people into the kingdom by sharing the true gospel, and by seeing them repent and be baptized as disciples of Christ. Every Christian is a minister (servant) of Jesus and has this ministry of reconciliation. This is how the Church is going to be truly built up, in numbers and in power. We must ask ourselves these questions... when was the last time I actually shared the true gospel with someone and led them to repentance? Am I really willing to take the time to pray for others? Do I have the courage to ask people I don't know—if I can pray for them when I am out at the mall, on the job or wherever people are around me? Do I really know how to share the gospel? Do I really expect to see people healed when I pray for them? Do I know how to get them free from demons and lead them to salvation through the gospel of Jesus Christ.

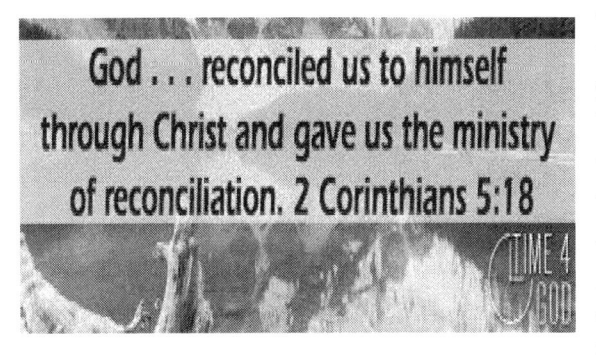

It is a very sad fact that many Christians cannot say yes to all of the above questions—not that they don't want to do these things—it is mainly because they have seldom, if ever been taught how to do these things. The mindset is "that it is the ministers job." No, their job is to train you to do these things—mainly because they have been doing these things themselves (a true minister will be doing these things by the way). Are we really ready to give up our "self-life" and truly make Jesus LORD by being obedient to what He said His followers must do? Those who are willing and obedient will move into experiencing the reality of what Jesus died for us to have. He wanted us to have the abundant life... a life that is daily filled with doing the exciting work of the ministry as He defined it in (Mark 16:15-18). Jesus is still asking His followers:

"But why do you call Me 'Lord, Lord,' and not do the things which I say? (Luke 6:46-48 NJKV)

2. You Must Be Baptized with the Holy Spirit

As we have discussed, being baptized with the Holy Spirit is an element needed for being born again, so we can walk in newness of life. Being *filled* or baptized with the Holy Spirit is part of the born-again experience. This is what gives us the power to do what Jesus said His disciples would do.

> **And He said to them, "Go into all the world and preach the gospel to every creature.**
>
> **He who believes and is baptized will be saved; but he who does not believe will be condemned.**
>
> **And these signs will follow those who believe: In My name they will cast out demons; they will speak with new tongues;**
>
> **they will take up serpents; and if they drink anything deadly, it will by no means hurt them; they will lay hands on the sick, and they will recover." (Mark 16:15-18) NKJV**

As we have mentioned, the new birth or being born again causes spiritual life (light) to be conceived within our human spirit. When we are baptized in water, we are making the commitment to make Jesus Lord of our lives by dying to the power of sin so we can be raised up to walk in newness of life.

When we are baptized in the Holy Spirit we become filled to overflowing, and are mantled with God's *supernatural power* that gives us the "can do" power or ability to live for Him and to serve Him.

Much false teaching has entered the church because of not understanding or believing what the Bible teaches on the subject of being baptized with the Holy Spirit.

Satan has attacked the doctrine of the Holy Spirit baptism with a vengeance—because he knows a Holy Spirit baptized person has supernatural power from God to overcome sin that can destroy Satan's works not only in them but also upon the earth.

We must let the word of God determine the truth on this subject and not our personal opinions or religious traditions and experiences. Being baptized with the Holy Spirit can be explained by using the following illustration.

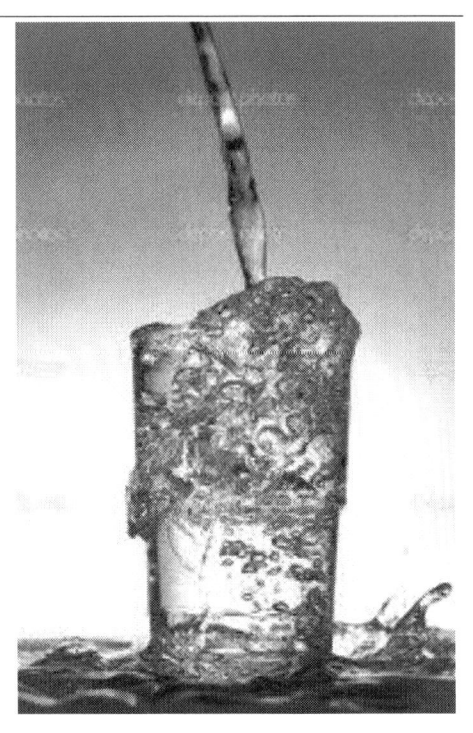

A glass, (representing a born again person), contains water (representing the Holy Spirit) thus filling the person when they are born again. But when the water flows over the brim completely filling and coming down ***upon*** **the** ***outside*** *and* covering the glass... then (the person), is not only filled with Holy Spirit—they have been *baptized (immersed-or covered) with the Holy Spirit*—because He has come upon them—through His overflowing presence.

In the book of Acts there is an account concerning a group of believers in Jesus who had not been *baptized in water in Jesus name*—and who also knew nothing about being *baptized in the Holy Spirit*. This means they had light from the Holy Spirit dwelling in them (water in their glass)—also meaning their candle (spirit) was lit by God through their faith in Jesus Christ and the indwelling of the Holy Spirit.

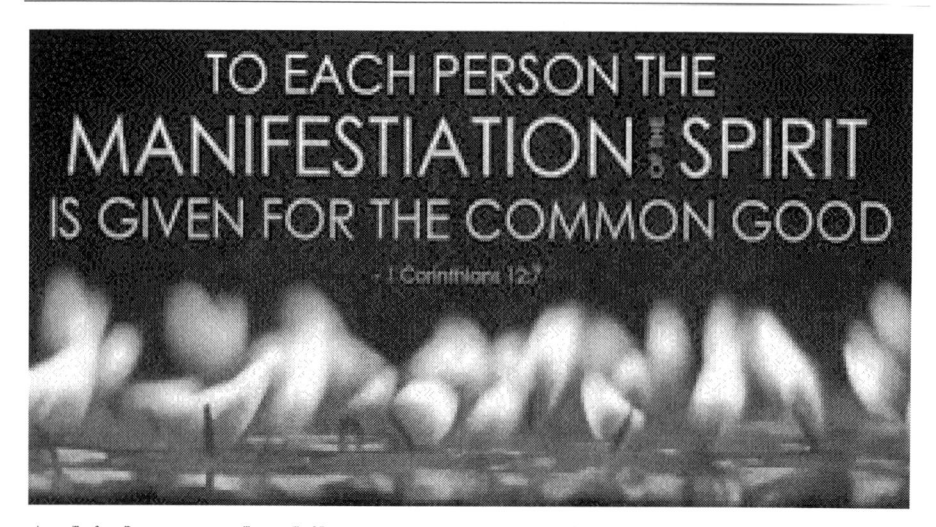

> **TO EACH PERSON THE MANIFESTIATION OF THE SPIRIT IS GIVEN FOR THE COMMON GOOD**
> *- 1 Corinthians 12:7*

And it happened, while Apollos was at Corinth, that Paul, having passed through the upper regions, came to Ephesus. And finding some disciples ... he said to them, "<u>**Did you receive the Holy Spirit when you believed?**</u>" So they said to him, "We have not so much as heard whether there is a Holy Spirit." ...And he said to them, "Into what then were you baptized?" So they said, "Into John's baptism." ...Then Paul said, "John indeed baptized with a baptism of repentance, saying to the people that they should believe on Him who would come after him, that is, on Christ Jesus." ...<u>**When they heard this, they were baptized in the name of the Lord Jesus**</u>... And when Paul had laid hands on them, the Holy Spirit came upon them, and they spoke with tongues and prophesied. (Acts 19:1-7) NKJV (Parenthesis mine).

Notice how quickly they obeyed and got baptized in water <u>in the name of Jesus</u>. In (verse 6) it says the Holy Spirit **came upon** these followers of Jesus after the Apostle Paul laid his hands upon them.

They then, received a baptism of supernatural power from God and immediately demonstrated that power by supernaturally <u>speaking in tongues</u> and also <u>prophesying</u>. These are only two of the *nine spiritual gifts of the Holy Spirit* that are mentioned in (1 Cor 12:7-10).

The Word of God clearly reveals that supernatural acts or manifestations known as *spiritual gifts* will be seen operating through those who receive this baptism of "dunamis power" from the Holy Spirit. These gifts are our tools for the work of the ministry.[2] Jesus said...

"**Behold, I send the Promise of My Father upon you; but tarry in the city of Jerusalem until you are endued[3] with power from on high.**" **(Luke 24:49) NKJV**

After the disciples had just witnessed Jesus being taken up to heaven, 120 faithful followers gathered together in the upper room to *tarry* or wait in Jerusalem for the outpouring of the Holy Spirit as Jesus had promised them. Here are the last recorded words of Jesus...

But you will receive power when the Holy Spirit comes upon you; and you will be my witnesses in Jerusalem, and in all Judea and Samaria, and to the ends of the earth."
After he said this, he was taken up before their very eyes, and a cloud hid him from their sight.

---

[2] For a complete study on the subject of the gifts of the Holy Spirit, you may enroll in the FREE Spiritual Gifts Course on our website at **www.extendedlifeCTM.org** —you may also order or read the Spiritual Gifts Manual on line free of charge. For more information, see the advertisement pages at the end of this book for more of Karen's resources.

[3] The word "endued" is the Greek word (Strong's 1746) ***enduo*** (en-doo'-o); which means: to have something put upon one as a covering i.e. in this case it is the POWER from the Holy Spirit baptism.

They were looking intently up into the sky as he was going, when suddenly two men dressed in white stood beside them.

"Men of Galilee," they said, "why do you stand here looking into the sky? This same Jesus, who has been taken from you into heaven, will come back in the same way you have seen him go into heaven." (Acts 1:8-11) NIV

The prophet Joel, in the Old Testament, prophesied hundreds of years before the birth of Jesus, that in the end times the Holy Spirit would be poured out upon (or baptize) God's people. As a result, they would manifest supernatural gifts from the Holy Spirit. This came to pass on the day of the Jewish festival known as Pentecost, which was seven weeks after Jesus had been resurrected. Here is the account of what happened on that day while they were waiting for the promise of the Holy Spirit...

When the day of Pentecost came, they were all together in one place.

Suddenly a sound like the blowing of a violent wind came from heaven and filled the whole house where they were sitting.

They saw what seemed to be tongues of fire that separated and came to rest on each of them.

All of them were filled with the Holy Spirit and began to speak in other tongues as the Spirit enabled them.

When they heard this sound, a crowd came together in bewilderment, because each one heard them speaking in his own language.

Amazed and perplexed, they asked one another, "What does this mean?"

Some, however, made fun of them and said, "They have had too much wine."

Then Peter stood up with the Eleven, raised his voice and addressed the crowd: "Fellow Jews and all of you who live in Jerusalem, let me explain this to you; listen carefully to what I say.

No, this is what was spoken by the prophet Joel:
"'In the last days, God says, I will pour out my Spirit on all people. Your sons and daughters will prophesy, your young men will see visions, your old men will dream dreams.

Even on my servants, both men and women, I will pour out my Spirit in those days, and they will prophesy. (Acts 2:1-4, 6, 12-14, 16-18) NIV

If we are true disciples this promise is also for us. How do we know that for sure? Because Jesus said His disciples would be witnesses or living proof of this power—in Jerusalem (which happened on the day of Pentecost as we just read) and also to—the ends of the earth.

The first disciples of the early church did not go to the ends of the earth in their day — but we are doing so in our day! That is how we know that this promise is for every born-again believer who is a true disciple of Jesus Christ. Here again, is what Jesus said to His disciples about the *baptism of the Holy Spirit.*

John baptized with water, but... you will be baptized with the Holy Spirit.

When the Spirit <u>comes upon you</u>, you will receive *[dunamis]* <u>power</u> and <u>you shall be my witnesses</u> in Jerusalem, and in all Judea and Samaria, and <u>to the ends of the earth</u>." (Acts 1:5, 8) NIV

WHEN THE HOLY SPIRIT EMPOWERS THE BELIEVER

The word power in the Greek text as it is used in (vs. 8) above is ***dunamis,*** and it literally means ***supernatural-can do ability***. This kind of supernatural ability is needed to live the kind of life Jesus called us to live and to do the supernatural acts he commanded His followers to do.

Therefore, our godly lives and the supernatural acts we do in His name, will bear witness to the fact that we have been baptized in the Holy Spirit. When you study the book of Acts you will find that those who were baptized in the Holy Spirit manifested a supernatural gift from the Holy Spirit.

And these signs shall follow them that believe; In my name they shall cast out devils; they shall speak with new tongues...They shall take up serpents; and if they drink any deadly thing, it shall not hurt them; they shall lay hands on the sick, and they shall recover. (Mark 16:17-18) KJV

Spiritual Gifts

Jesus told His followers, because He was going back to the Father, He would send the Holy Spirit who would also be our counsellor and comforter...

And I will ask the Father, and he will give you another Comforter and Counselor, who will never leave you...He is the Holy Spirit, who leads into all truth. The world at large cannot receive him, because it isn't looking for him and doesn't recognize him. But you do, because he lives... in you. (John 14:16-17) NLT

Jesus died so we could be partakers of His *divine nature*. That nature includes not only His godly character but also His supernatural abilities.

And by that same mighty (dunamis) **power, he has given us all of his rich and wonderful promises. He has promised that you will escape the decadence all around you caused by evil desires and that you will share in his divine nature. (2 Peter 1:4) NLT** (Parenthesis mine).

There are those who teach that supernatural acts and the spiritual gifts ceased to operate when the founding apostles of the Church who are mentioned in the books of Acts died. There is, however, no Biblical basis for such a teaching. *(This false teaching is known as the doctrine of "cessation" and is thoroughly examined in the Spiritual Gifts Manual. For more information on this manual—see the last page of this book).*

Because our God is a supernatural God, He has given His people supernatural abilities called *spiritual gifts*, so we can be effective witnesses and ministers to others. When we are born again we become members of Christ's body, known as the church. Each body member has been ordained by God to receive the evidence of the Holy Spirit's baptism through the manifestation of the spiritual gifts they are given—thus they can function in their part of the body of Christ and fulfil their ministry of serving others.

And now, dear brothers and sisters, I will write about the special abilities the Holy Spirit gives to each of us. NLT

Now there are distinctive varieties and distributions of gifts—extraordinary powers — and they vary, but the same Holy Spirit.
And there are distinctive varieties of service, but it is the same Lord Who is served.
And there are distinctive varieties of operation, but it is the same God Who inspires and energizes them all in all.

But to each one is given the manifestation of the Holy Spirit— as evidence—of the Spirit for good and profit. (1 Corinthians 12:1, 4-7)
AMP

The Apostle Peter in the text below also affirms we are to receive the baptism of the Holy Spirit. Notice this is to happen *after* we turn from our sins and are baptized in water in Jesus name as a true disciple.

Spiritual Gifts List

Peter replied, "Each of you must <u>turn from your sins and turn to God</u>, and be <u>baptized in the name of Jesus Christ</u> for the remission of (deliverance from) your sins. <u>Then you will receive the GIFT of the Holy Spirit</u>. This promise is to you and to your children, and even to the Gentiles—all who have been called by the Lord our God." (Acts 2:38-39) NLT

In the text just quoted, the Apostle Peter called the baptism in the Holy Spirit a *gift*. God does not force His gifts on anyone, such as the gift called "eternal Life" (Rom 6:23). We must be willing to receive God's gifts by faith. In order to receive *the gift of the Holy Spirit baptism,* we must believe this gift is for us.

We must be willing to believe and to receive it the same way we received *the gift of eternal life* when we are born again. It is by faith that we receive Jesus as Lord and Savior of our life and it is also by faith that we receive the gift of God's Holy Spirit.

According to your faith be it unto you. (Matthew 9:29) KJV

This means we must have faith in the *message* or word spoken by Jesus and His Apostles regarding these wonderful gifts from God. When we receive the Holy Spirit by faith, the Scriptures, as we have seen, tell us He will manifest His supernatural gifts through us, <u>according to our faith</u>…

So then <u>faith come by hearing</u>, and <u>hearing by the word of God</u>. (Romans 10:17) NKJV

Receiving the Baptism of the Holy Spirit

When seeking to receive the baptism of the Holy Spirit Keep in mind these things…

- When those in the Bible that were baptized or filled (furnished) with the Holy Spirit **THEY DID THE SPEAKING** (Luke 1:67, Acts 2:4) ... Therefore, you must open your mouth and <u>you must do the speaking</u>! The Biblical pattern for speaking is one or all of these ...

*SPEAKING IN TONGUES (Acts 2:4, 11, 10:46)

*PRAISING GOD (Acts 10:46)

*PROPHESYING (Acts 19:6)

Whatever words you get from God when the Holy Spirit comes upon you, YOU MUST DO THE SPEAKING...

And when they had prayed, the place was shaken where they were assembled together; and they were all filled (furnished) with the Holy Spirit, and they spoke the word of (from) God with boldness. (Acts 4:31) KJV

- Don't allow your mind to get in the way... The Bible says the speaking gift of other tongues can be that of men (a human language) or a language of angels (a language not known to humans) ... the Apostle Paul said:

I speak with the tongues of men and of angels... (1 Cor 13:11)

Therefore, unless you understand every language of man, and angels, *you will not understand what you are speaking.* It is your spirit man that is speaking through the power of the Holy Spirit upon you. Your natural mind has nothing to do with speaking a language given by the Holy Spirit.

For if I pray in a tongue, my spirit prays, but my understanding is unfruitful. (1 Cor 14:14)

Demonic spirits speak to our soul or our conscious mind...so they may try to distract you by giving you thoughts to keep you from SPEAKING out any kind of sound or foreign sounding words, by telling you "Oh that's just you speaking that!" Remember faith requires a response to what you believe. Faith requires actions. If you believe God is giving you a speaking gift, you must do the speaking! The Apostle Paul said:

And since we have the same spirit of faith, according to what is written, "I believed and therefore I spoke," we also believe and therefore speak. (2 Cor 4:13) NKJV

Sometimes the gifts of prophecy and speaking in other tongues (languages) came through the gift being imparted by the laying on of hands as in (Acts 19:6). There were times when those who had spiritual gifts, as demonstrated by the Apostle Paul, imparted gifts to others by the laying on of hands while praying for them.

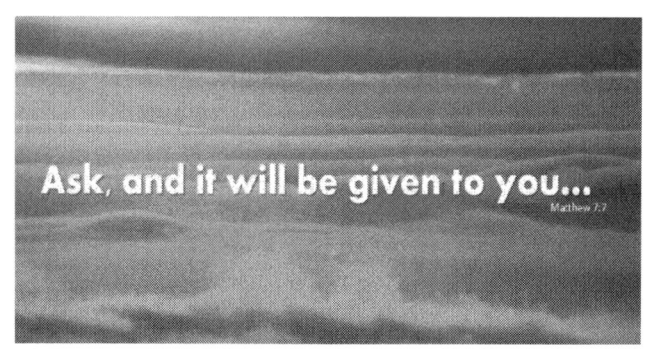

However, there were instances when people had the Holy Spirit come upon them without the laying on of hands (Act 10:45-46).

So you don't need to have anyone present to lay hands upon you in order to receive the gift of the Holy Spirit. I have known many who have received this gift in their bedroom or some other place while praying and asking God for it. If you desire to receive the gift of the Holy Spirit's power and believe God wants you to have it, just pray a simple prayer and ask God for this gift. Then be confident that what comes out of your mouth is a speaking gift from His Holy Spirit. If you ask you will receive...... **how much more will your heavenly Father give the Holy Spirit to those who ask him." (Luke 11:13)** • How do you know that what you are speaking has been given to you by God? Anything we ask God in faith will be given to us (Matthew 21:22; Mark 11:24; 1 Timothy 2:8; Hebrews 11:6). Remember faith comes by hearing and hearing by the word of God. Therefore, if God has spoken to your heart from His written word and convinced you that He wants to mantle you with the power of His Holy Spirit, you must be willing to accept the gift being offered to you. If you ask God Your Father for the gift of the Holy Spirit, then you must open your mouth and begin speaking and believe that He has given you what you asked for. He will not give you anything false, when you desire what is true…

"You fathers — if your children ask for a fish, do you give them a snake instead? ... Or if they ask for an egg, do you give them a scorpion? Of course not! ...If you sinful people know how to give good gifts to your children, how much more will your heavenly Father give the Holy Spirit to those who ask him." (Luke 11:11-13) NLT

Speaking Gift Activation Prayer

Are you ready... to receive an impartation from the Holy Spirit and be activated in your speaking gift? If you are ready... to believe and receive simply pray something like this...

Dear Heavenly Father... I have by faith received your gift of eternal life, and now I deeply desire the gift of being baptized with your Holy Spirit. I need His power in my life, and I desire to demonstrate through His power your gifts, so I can confirm your word with signs and wonders to those who need to hear Your gospel. I am convinced the baptism of the Holy Spirit is for me, and that you want to give it to me. I fully expect that the Holy Spirit will come upon me and impart whatever speaking gifts He desires to give me. I thank you now that you are imparting this gift to me... and I receive it now by faith in Your word. I ask all these things in the name of Jesus Christ my Lord and Savior. Amen

Now open your mouth and remember you must start speaking... it may be in an unknown language that has no meaning to you or you may sing out your praises to God! In any case—you must do the speaking!

For if I pray in a tongue, <u>my spirit prays</u>, but my understanding is unfruitful... What is the conclusion then? I will pray with the spirit...I will <u>sing with the spirit</u>. (1 Cor 14:14-15) NKJV

3. Become a Sanctified Believer

In the above text we are told that the bride of Christ—known as the church—is a *sanctified* (pure and holy) church. All who have been born again were sanctified by the blood of Jesus at that the time of their spiritual birth. However, we must allow the Holy Spirit to continually do the work of *sanctification* in our lives, so we stay pure and holy before God. Only those who *allow God's sanctifying work* are qualified to be called a *saint*. Sanctification is a daily process where we are cleansed by the blood of Jesus through confessing any sin that the Word of God reveals in our lives.

Therefore, Jesus also, <u>that He might sanctify the people with His own blood</u>, suffered outside the gate. (Hebrews 13:12) NKJV

...Christ also loved the church, and gave himself for it;
That <u>he might sanctify and cleanse it</u> with the washing of water <u>by the word</u>,
That he might present it to himself a <u>glorious church</u>, not having spot, or wrinkle, or any such thing; but that it should be <u>holy and without blemish</u>. (Ephesians 5:25-27) KJV

The above text tells us that Jesus is going to be presented with a *glorious* bride (church). In order for this to be the case— His people must be sanctified by being *washed* by the water of His Word.

For the word of God is living and powerful... (Hebrews 4:12) NKJV

The words *sanctify* and *saint* both come from the same Greek word, which is—***hagios*** (hag'-ee-os), which means *pure, blameless, saints.* Living by the word of God will accomplish this in our lives.

Now may the God of peace Himself sanctify you completely; and may your whole spirit, soul, and body be preserved blameless at the coming of our Lord Jesus Christ. (1 Thessalonians 5:23) NKJV

To insure that we are seen as *blameless* of all sin in God's eyes we must remain *justified* (innocent)—by being *sanctified* (cleansed)—so we can become *glorified* (transformed) for eternity.

The Glorified Saints

The Bible also tells us that Jesus is coming back to take His Bride— the church (the saints) out of this world to dwell with Him for eternity. We are going to meet Jesus in the air and when this happens our *mortal physical body*—will be changed instantly—as in the twinkling of an eye—into an immortal, resurrected *glorified* body, like the resurrected glorified body of Jesus Christ.

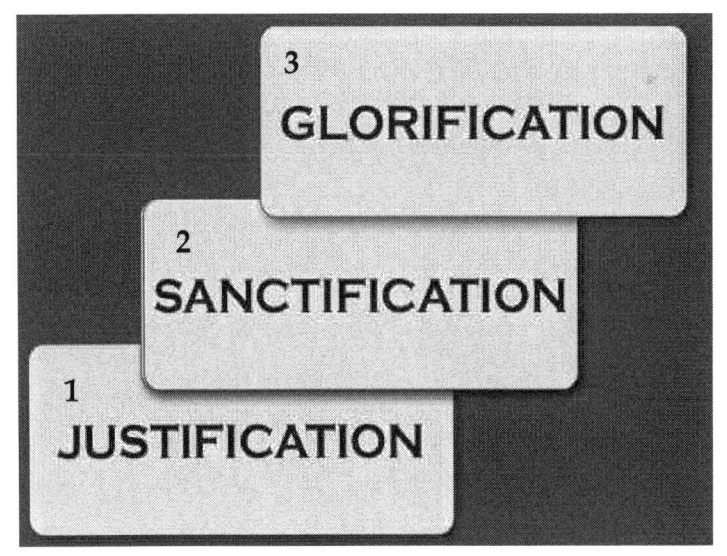

3. GLORIFICATION
2. SANCTIFICATION
1. JUSTIFICATION

> **For the Lord himself will come down from heaven with a commanding shout, with the call of the archangel, and with the trumpet call of God. First, all the Christians who have died will rise from their graves...**
> **Then, together with them, we who are still alive and remain on the earth will be caught up in the clouds to meet the Lord in the air and remain with him forever...**
> **So comfort and encourage each other with these words. (1 Thessalonians 4:16-18) NLT**

It is at this "meeting in the air" at the first resurrection—often called the rapture, that we will be changed instantly and receive our glorified body.

> **It will happen in a moment, in the blinking of an eye, when the last trumpet is blown. For when the trumpet sounds, the Christians who have died will be raised with transformed (glorified) bodies. And then we who are living will be transformed (glorified) so that we will never die.**

For our perishable earthly bodies must be transformed into heavenly bodies that will never die. When this happens — when our perishable earthly bodies have been transformed into heavenly bodies that will never die—"Death is swallowed up in victory. (1 Corinthians 15:52-54) NLT (Parenthesis mine).

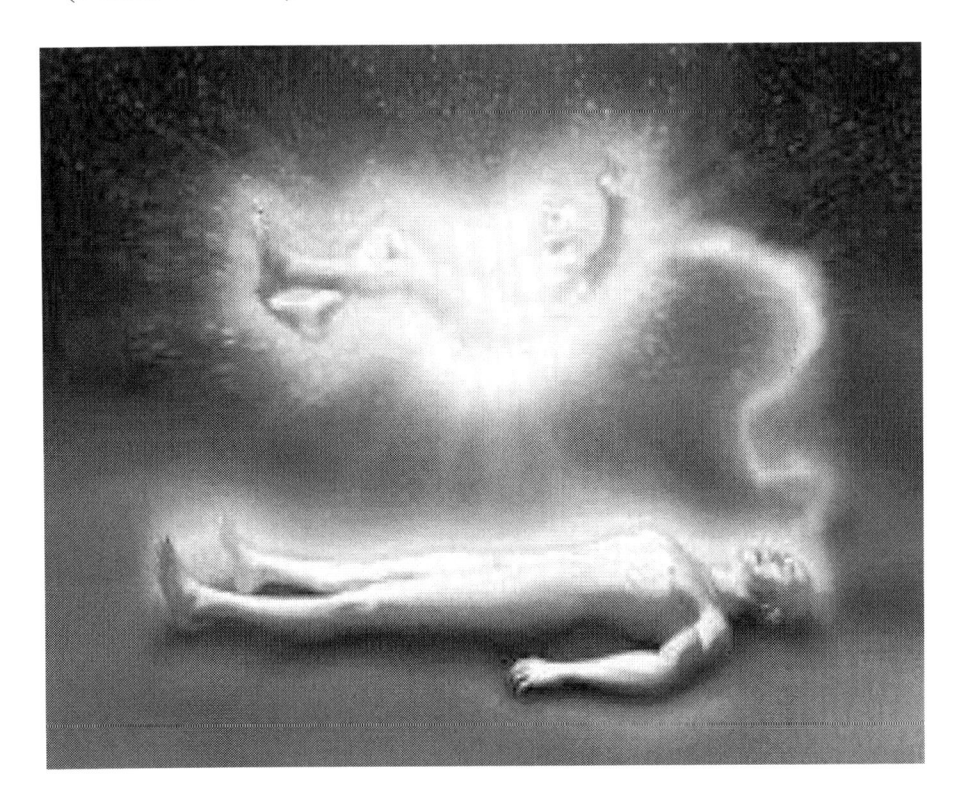

And I saw thrones, and they sat on them, and judgment was committed to them. Then I saw the souls of those who had been beheaded for their witness to Jesus and for the word of God, who had not worshiped the beast or his image, and had not received his mark on their foreheads or on their hands. And they lived and reigned with Christ for a thousand years.

But the rest of the dead did not live again until the thousand years were finished. This is the first resurrection.

> **Blessed and holy is he who has part in the first resurrection. Over such the second death has no power, but they shall be priests of God and of Christ, and shall reign with Him a thousand years. (Revelation 20:4-6) NKJV**

We can get a glimpse of what this new resurrected body will be like, because after Jesus was resurrected from the dead, he appeared to His disciples in his new resurrected body.

In His new body He was not confined to the physical laws our body is now subject to. In his new body He could touch things in the natural or physical realm but He could also disappear into the spiritual realm when He wanted to. In the following account we find Jesus walking with the disciples when he appeared to them after he had risen from the dead...

> **By this time they were nearing Emmaus and the end of their journey. Jesus would have gone on... but they begged him to stay the night with them, since it was getting late. So he went home with them... As they sat down to eat, he took a small loaf of bread, asked God's blessing on it, broke it, then gave it to them... Suddenly, their eyes were opened, and they recognized him. <u>And at that moment he disappeared</u>! ... They said to each other, "Didn't our hearts feel strangely warm as he talked with us on the road and explained the Scriptures to us?" And within the hour they were on their way back to Jerusalem, where the eleven disciples and the other followers of Jesus were gathered. When they arrived, they were greeted with the report..."The Lord has really risen! He appeared to Peter!" (Luke 24:28-34) NLT**

> ...when he shall appear, we shall be like him; for we shall see him as he is.
> 1 John 3:2b

In the above account you will notice that Jesus appeared to look like an ordinary human person who could *handle bread* yet simply disappear at will. This then, is how our glorified bodies will be also. We will be able to function in the earthly realm, but also function as a spiritual being just as Jesus did.

We have so much to look forward to—if we remain blameless in this life through the sanctifying power of God's work in our lives. We must work hard at keeping our lives free from sin in order to bring honor to God and not disgrace upon the Lord's name. If we are going to call ourselves a Christian, we must be *Christ-like*. We do this through studying God's word and listening to the Holy Spirit when He speaks to our hearts about any sin issues that need to be confessed and cleansed by the blood of Jesus. This way we can be sure of being part of the blameless Bride of Christ.

So, my dear brothers and sisters, remain strong and steady, always enthusiastic about the Lord's work... for you know that nothing you do for the Lord is ever useless. (1 Corinthians 15:58) NLT

As we can see God has special favor and blessings awaiting those who are willing to prepare themselves to be part of the Bride of Christ. That is why it is important to allow God to get us ready.

So be prepared, because you don't know what day your Lord is coming. You also must be ready all the time. For the Son of Man will come when least expected. (Matthew 24:42) NLT

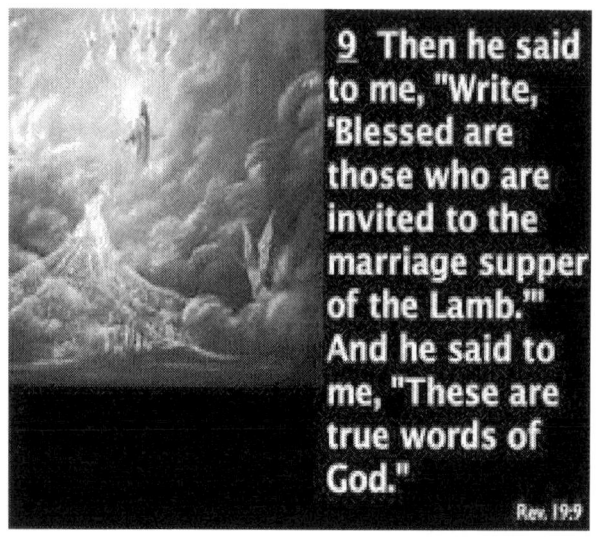

> **9** Then he said to me, "Write, 'Blessed are those who are invited to the marriage supper of the Lamb.'" And he said to me, "These are true words of God."
> Rev. 19:9

Our reunion with Jesus when He comes back to get us at the first resurrection, for all His true followers, will be a time of great celebration, called a wedding feast... or the "Marriage Supper of the Lamb."

We do not know the day or the hour that Jesus is coming back to take us out of this world, which is why we must always be prepared for this time of celebration. Many, I'm sad to say, who are born again <u>will not be ready for His return</u>—because they were not serious about allowing God to *sanctify them*—which means they failed to <u>put on their wedding garment called the new man</u> who is clothed with righteousness and holiness—as we discussed previously. Those who did not prepare themselves (by putting on their wedding garment) will not be allowed to be part of the glorious bride of Christ and her "wedding celebration" (reunion with Jesus) that our Heavenly Father has prepared for us...

"The Kingdom of Heaven can be illustrated by the story of a king who prepared a great wedding feast for his son...

But when the king came in to meet the guests, he noticed a man who wasn't wearing the proper clothes for a wedding.

'Friend,' he asked, 'how is it that you are here without <u>wedding clothes</u>?' And the man had no reply.

Then the king said to his aides, 'Bind him hand and foot and throw him out into the outer darkness, where there is weeping and gnashing of teeth.'

For many are called, but few are chosen." (Matthew 22:2, 11-14) NLT

Being Prepared for the End-Times

Jesus also warned we must be prepared for a time of great trouble and sorrow that would come upon the earth in the end-time—before He comes back to set up His earthly kingdom. Here is what Jesus said...

And wars will break out near and far, but don't panic. Yes, these things must come, but the end won't follow immediately.
The nations and kingdoms will proclaim war against each other, and there will be famines and earthquakes in many parts of the world... But all this will be only the beginning of the horrors to come... "Then you will be arrested, persecuted, and killed. You will be hated all over the world because of your allegiance to me... And many will turn away from me and betray and hate each other... And many false prophets and false teachers will appear and will lead many people astray... Sin will be rampant everywhere, and the love of many will grow cold... But those who endure to the end will be saved... And the Good News about the Kingdom will be preached throughout the whole world, so that all nations will hear it; and then, finally, the end will come.

...For that will be a time of greater horror than anything the world has ever seen or will ever see again... In fact, unless that time of calamity is shortened, the entire human race will be destroyed. But it will be shortened for the sake of God's chosen ones. (Matthew 24:6-14, 21-22) NLT

Jesus said, for the sake of His saints, the chosen born again ones on earth, He would shorten their time of tribulation on earth. This means the true Christians will not be on earth when the last seven judgments (known as bowl or vial judgments—depending on your Bible translation) are poured out upon the wicked. These last seven judgments are known as "The Day of the Lord." The true saints of God are resurrected at the "7th or last trumpet judgment[4], as Paul mentioned in the following texts:

In a moment, in the twinkling of an eye, at the <u>last</u> (7th) trumpet. For the trumpet will sound, and the dead will be raised incorruptible, and we shall be changed. (1 Cor 15:52) NKJV

---

[4] You can read about the seven seal, seven trumpet and seven bowl judgments that take place during the tribulation period in (Rev chapters 6-16).

> And another angel came out of the temple, crying with a loud voice to Him who sat on the cloud, "Thrust in Your sickle and reap, for the time has come for You to reap, for the harvest of the earth is ripe." So He who sat on the cloud thrust in His sickle on the earth, and the earth was reaped. (Rev 14:15-16) NKJV

After this horrible time of the last seven bowl judgments known as the Great Tribulation—Jesus will return with his mighty army of angels and resurrected, glorified saints to destroy the enemies of God who are upon the earth. His saints will then rule with Jesus for 1000 years as kings and priests over all the people of the earth who live through the awful period of great tribulation. (Read Matthew 24).

> Then I saw heaven opened, and a white horse was standing there. And the one sitting on the horse (Jesus) was named Faithful and True. For he judges fairly and then goes to war... He was clothed with a robe dipped in blood, and his title was the <u>Word of God</u>... The armies of heaven (the saints and angels), dressed in <u>pure white linen</u>, followed him on white horses... From his mouth came a sharp sword, and with it he struck down the nations. He ruled them with an iron rod... On his robe and thigh was written this title: King of kings and Lord of lords. (Revelation 19:12-16) NLT

What a glorious time we have to look forward to! We who kept ourselves pure and blameless as the Saints of God—are going to rule with Jesus in His kingdom which He is going to establish upon the earth when He returns. He will also destroy His enemies when He comes back to earth.

And hath made us kings and priests unto God and his Father; to him be glory and dominion for ever and ever. Amen (Revelation 1:6)

(He) has made us unto our God kings and priests: and we shall reign on the earth. (Revelation 5:10) KJV

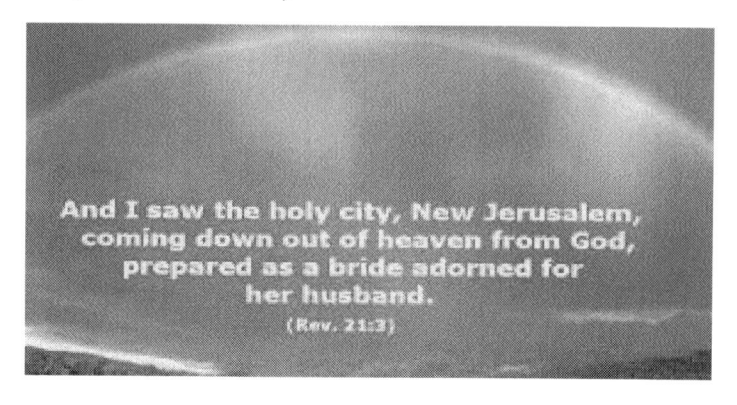

> And I saw the holy city, New Jerusalem, coming down out of heaven from God, prepared as a bride adorned for her husband.
> (Rev. 21:3)

Just imagine! All who are the born again, holy saints of God, are going to be rewarded their inheritance of being a king and priest upon the earth and after the 1000 years, that it will take for Jesus and His saints to establish His Kingdom reign upon earth, God is going to create a new heaven and a new earth that we will live in for eternity and the City of God called THE NEW JERUSALEM, will be the home of the Saints of God.

> **Now I saw a new heaven and a new earth, for the first heaven and the first earth had passed away. Also there was no more sea.**
>
> **Then I, John, saw the holy city, New Jerusalem, coming down out of heaven from God, prepared as a bride adorned for her husband.**
>
> **And I heard a loud voice from heaven saying, "Behold, the tabernacle of God is with men, and He will dwell with them, and they shall be His people. God Himself will be with them and be their God.**
>
> **And God will wipe away every tear from their eyes; there shall be no more death, nor sorrow, nor crying. There shall be no more pain, for the former things have passed away."**

> Then He who sat on the throne said, "Behold, I make all things new." And He said to me, "Write, for these words are true and faithful."
>
> Then one of the seven angels who had the seven bowls filled with the seven last plagues came to me and talked with me, saying, "Come, I will show you the bride, the Lamb's wife."
>
> And he carried me away in the Spirit to a great and high mountain, and showed me the great city, the holy Jerusalem, descending out of heaven from God,
>
> having the glory of God. Her light was like a most precious stone... **(Rev 21:1-5, 9-11) NKJV**

God's people will rule and reign with Christ upon the earth. The prophet Daniel saw thousands of years into the future and prophesied this very thing...

Until the Ancient of days (Jesus) **came, and judgment was given to the saints of the Most-High; and the time came that the saints possessed the kingdom... And the kingdom and dominion, and the greatness of the kingdom under the whole heaven, shall be given to the people of the saints of the Most-High, whose kingdom is an everlasting kingdom, and all dominions shall serve and obey him** (Jesus in His Kingdom). **(Daniel 7:22, 27) KJV** (Parenthesis

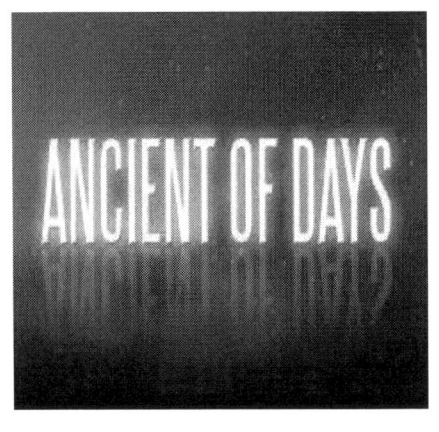

There will be great rejoicing for those who are ready for the return of Jesus for His Bride!

> **Then I heard again what sounded like the shout of a huge crowd, or the roar of mighty ocean waves, or the crash of loud thunder: "Hallelujah! For the Lord our God, the Almighty, reigns... Let us be glad and rejoice and honor him. <u>For the time has come for the wedding feast of the Lamb</u>, and <u>his bride has prepared herself</u>... She is permitted to wear the finest white linen." And the angel said, "Write this: ...Blessed are those who are invited to the wedding feast of the Lamb." And he added, "These are true words that come from God." (Revelation 19:6-9) NLT**

One can see by what I have written in this book that—simply calling yourself a Christian will not prepare you to be part of the church (the body and bride of Christ). <u>We must be committed to following Jesus by obeying His word on a daily basis</u>. Otherwise we may these awful words:

Many will say to Me in that day, 'Lord, Lord, have we not prophesied in Your name, cast out demons in Your name, and done many wonders in Your name?' ...And then I will declare to them, 'I never knew you; depart from Me, you who practice lawlessness!' (Matthew 7:22-23) NKJV

4.

Find a Bible Believing Fellowship

It is so important to become part of a Christian family (local fellowship). Just as new born babies need their parents and other family members to help them develop in a healthy way, we also need a spiritual family.

For where two or three are gathered together in My name, I am there in the midst of them." (Matthew 18:20) NKJV

Fellowship with other true Christians is vital and <u>we must be committed to meeting with other Christians of like mind and of like faith</u>—who can not only help and encourage us, but also warn us and keep us on track if we are headed in the wrong direction.

<u>And let us not neglect our meeting together</u>, as some people do, but <u>encourage</u> and <u>warn each other</u>, especially now that the day of his coming back again is drawing near. (Hebrews 10:25) NLT

The body (family) of Christ is God's dwelling place in which we find not only comfort and encouragement, but also agreement in prayer for deliverance and healing for our spirit, soul and body.

In the coming end times we will need each other more than ever in order survive the coming times of famine and distress. It is in a God's fellowships we find:

4...rejoicing in his presence! 5 (we find a) **Father to the fatherless, a defender of widows — this is God, whose dwelling is holy. 6 God places the lonely in families; he sets the prisoners free and gives them joy. But for rebels** (those who refuse to gather with other believers), **there is only famine and distress. (Psalms 68:4-6) NLT**

God places us in spiritual families so we are protected from our enemies (Satan and his demons). Some Christians meet in church buildings, other gather together in home fellowships. Where ever they meet, there must be leaders who are called by God to shepherd God's people. <u>Our pastors and other spiritual leaders in the local church gatherings are there to give us spiritual oversight through their instruction, counsel and correction— in order to keep us safe and spiritually healthy</u>.

Obey your spiritual leaders and do what they say. Their work is to watch over your souls, and they know they are accountable to God. Give them reason to do this joyfully and not with sorrow. That would certainly not be for your benefit. (Hebrews 13:17) NLT

It is imperative find a Bible believing and preaching, Christian spiritual family that puts the Word of God above the philosophies and traditions of man. Listen to what Jesus said to a religious leader of His day...

These people honor me with their lips, but their hearts are far away. Their worship is a farce, for they replace God's commands with their own man-made teachings... 'For you ignore God's (word) and substitute your own traditions." ...Then he said, "You reject God's (word) in order to hold on to your own traditions. (Mark 7:7-9) NLT

God has ordained spiritual leaders to also help us find our particular place in the body of Christ, known as His universal church. When we are born again we have a particular place and function to fulfil in the church, which is the body of Christ...

Understanding the Body of Christ

Being in relationship through fellowship with other true believers means they help us and we help them. Just as we need every part of our own physical body, so it is we also need all the <u>members </u>of Christ's body— in order to function in our Christian life.

God has supernatural gifts and abilities that he gives to each of us who become members of His Body by being born-again. This is so we can function as part of His body within the church...

...But we have all been baptized into Christ's body by one Spirit, and we have all received the same Spirit.
Yes, <u>the body has many different parts</u>, not just one part.
If the foot says, "I am not a part of the body because I am not a hand," that does not make it any less a part of the body.
And if the ear says, "I am not part of the body because I am only an ear and not an eye," would that make it any less a part of the body? Suppose the whole body was an eye--then how would you hear? Or if your whole body were just one big ear, how could you smell anything?

But God made our bodies with many parts, and he has put each part just where he wants it.
What a strange thing a body would be if it had only one part!
Yes, there are many parts, but only one body.
The eye can never say to the hand, "I don't need you." The head can't say to the feet, "I don't need you."
In fact, some of the parts that seem weakest and least important are really the most necessary.
This makes for harmony among the members, so that all the members care for each other equally.
If one part suffers, all the parts suffer with it, and if one part is honored, all the parts are glad.
Now all of you together are Christ's body, and each one of you is a separate and necessary part of it.
Here is a list of some of the members that God has placed in the body of Christ...
first are apostles,
second are prophets,
third are teachers,
then those who do miracles,
those who have the gift of healing,
those who can help others,
those who can get others to work together,
those who speak in unknown languages.
Is everyone an apostle? Of course not. Is everyone a prophet? No. Are all teachers? Does everyone have the power to do miracles? Does everyone have the gift of healing? Of course not. Does God give all of us the ability to speak in unknown languages? Can everyone interpret unknown languages? No!
And in any event, you should desire the (best or) most helpful gifts.
NLT (1 Corinthians 12:13-22, 25-31)

The gifts God gives us are for doing the work of the ministry which is for the purpose of helping others and for building up the church.

You can read about the different members of Christ's body and how they function by carefully reviewing (verses 28-31) of this same chapter. (These functions are thoroughly examined in the Spiritual Gifts Manual offered by our ministry free of charge).

5.

Develop a Daily Bible Study Plan

In order to have strong faith so we can remain faithful to God, it is crucial that you find time each day to study the Bible. You must expect the Holy Spirit to speak to you as you read God's Word. This is how your faith will grow. Remember, as the Bible says, **_faith comes by hearing, and this means hearing from the word of God_**. In order for that to happen you must spend time reading and studying His Word.

The Bible is not like any other book. Therefore, you don't read it like any other book. Most people start reading a book at the beginning. However, in the Old Testament the first five books of the Bible are known as the *Torah* or the *law* of God. Then there are the books of Israel's history with God.

As important as it is to understand these books, my suggestion is that you first start by reading a chapter a day from the book of Psalms and Proverbs, which are also found in the Old Testament.

> These books were written to give us wisdom and insight concerning God and his dealings with us as human beings. *(For a complete overview of every book of the Bible we offer our FREE On-Line-Bible Study course— Which can also be mailed to you. For more information, see the resource information page at the end of this book).*

It is important that you also read from the New Testament Gospels (Matthew—Mark—Luke—John). I suggest starting with the Gospel of John and book of Acts, in order to gain insight into the Christian life and teachings of Jesus. Then go on to the books known as the *Epistles*, starting with the book of Romans, and continuing on to the book of Jude. Also read daily from the books of Psalms and Proverbs.

These books were written to believers so they could become strong in their new life as followers of Jesus Christ.

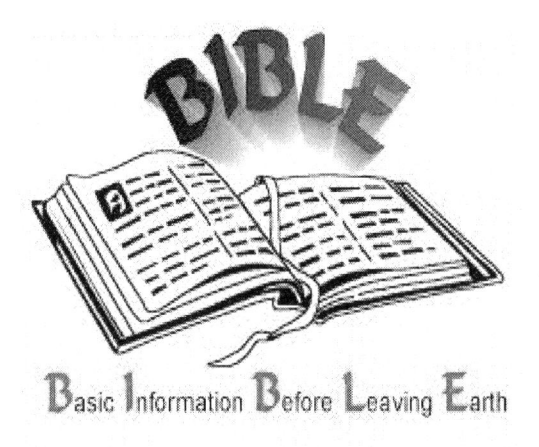

The Holy Spirit is and Must Be Your Teacher

As you read the Bible <u>*ask the Holy Spirit to speak to you*</u> about what you are reading and how it applies to you and your new life as a Christian. What you read will help you with what you must deal with on a daily basis. As you spend time reading and studying, you will grow in your understanding through God's Spirit of wisdom and knowledge.

Oh, the depth of the riches both of the wisdom and knowledge of God! (Romans 11:33) NKJV

<u>You must take the time to ponder and meditate on what you are reading</u>. You will be surprised at what you hear God whisper in your heart. When the prophet Elijah was looking for God he found that God's voice is called a *"still small voice"* ...

...but the LORD was not in the wind: and after the wind an earthquake; but the LORD was not in the earthquake. ...And after the earthquake a fire; but the LORD was not in the fire: and after the fire <u>a still small voice</u>... And it was so, when Elijah heard it... And, behold, there came a voice unto him, and said, what are you doing here, Elijah? (1 Kings 19:11-13) KJV

Our Spiritual growth is dependent upon spending time in God's word so we can hear His voice. His word will <u>instruct</u> us, <u>correct</u> us and guide <u>us</u> into the abundant life that Jesus died to give us.

In order for God to transform our life and make all things new, He must transform our way of thinking. Our thinking must line up with the word of God.

And be not conformed to this world: but be transformed by the <u>renewing of your mind</u>, that you may prove what is the good, and acceptable, and perfect, will of God. (Romans 12:2) NKJV

I try to encourage those who are serious about wanting to hear God speak to them from His word to look up the *key words* in the Bible verses being meditated upon, by using a Hebrew—Greek Bible Dictionary called the *Strong's Concordance,* which is keyed to the King James Bible.

Every English word used in the King James Bible can be found in their original Greek, Aramaic and Hebrew meanings. The Original manuscripts for the Old Testament were written in Hebrew and Aramaic, and the New Testament manuscripts were written in Greek.

You don't have to be a Hebrew or Greek scholar to understand the word meanings, from the Bible, in their original languages. As you look up the meanings to these words and meditate on what these words mean, the Holy Spirit will give you a deeper insight and greater revelation from God's word. Many false teachings concerning the Bible have invaded Christianity because Bible teachers did not have a full understanding of what the Word of God says. Those in error do not take the time to really study the Bible and understand the **manifold meanings** of God's word.

To the intent that now... might be known by the church the manifold wisdom of God. (Ephesians 3:10) KJV

> **Blessed is the person whose delight and desire are in the precepts, the instructions, the teachings of God; he habitually meditates, ponders and studies, by day and by night. (Ps 1:2) AMP**

That is why one verse of Scripture can have *manifold* or many applications of truth. Each application is an aspect of God's truth. These different applications and aspects of God's truth are again known as—God's *manifold wisdom* that is revealed to us from the Holy Spirit who breathes His inspiration upon the written word.

The Holy Spirit is the one who reveals each aspect of truth as we study and meditate on God's Word with a sincere desire to know the truth. The different aspects of truth found in Scripture verses will never however, contradict truths found in other verses of Scripture, instead they will reinforce compliment and harmonize with one another *(See the next chapter for more on this subject)*.

<u>Study</u> to show thyself approved unto God, a workman that need not be ashamed, <u>rightly dividing the word of truth</u>. (2 Timothy 2:15) KJV

The phrase *rightly dividing* literally means in the Greek text… *correctly dissecting* the Word of truth. When students in a science class dissect something, they take it apart and study each aspect of that part, in order to understand the whole thing, they are looking at.

That is what we must do with the *key words* used in Scripture if we want to receive the *manifold wisdom* of God's Word. When we look at all the different shades of meanings for the words God chose to put in the Bible—in the original languages of the Bible—the Holy Spirit paints a wonderfully detailed picture that results in a clearer understanding of what He is teaching us.

We should not rely solely upon people to teach us truth from the Bible. Not to say that God does not use people to teach us, He most certainly does. Teachers are one of the leadership gifts mentioned in (Ephesians 4:11).

Born-again followers of Jesus however, will be able to know or recognize the truth when they hear it.

It will witness to their spirit, where the light and life of God resides. If we are not born- again and do not have God's light and life within our spirit (as previously discussed) …we will not know the difference between truth and error when we hear it.

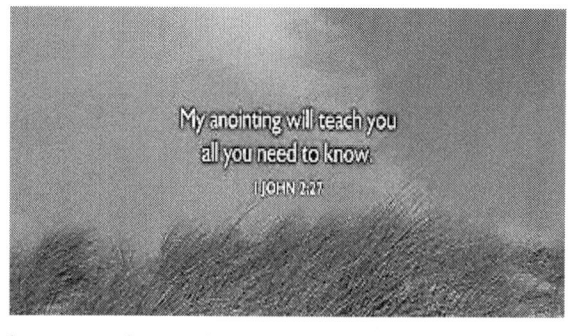

That is why many people believe wrong things from the Bible or about the Bible. They do not have the life giving anointing of the Holy Spirit in their spirit to teach them the difference between the truth and error. Thus they form opinions and beliefs that are not according to the truth from God's word.

> **But you** (who we are born again) **have an unction from the Holy One, and you know all things.**
> **But the anointing which you have received of him abides in you, and you need not that any man teach you: but as the same anointing teaches you of all things, and is truth, and is no lie, and even as it has taught you, you shall abide in him. (1 John 2:20, 27) KJV** (Parenthesis mine).

At first error only appears as a lane change
Proverbs 14:2

APOSTASY

We must treasure our spiritual life and gifts and not allow the devil to steal them, defile them or counterfeit them through embracing false teaching, all because we lack the knowledge of God's truth. This ignorance can lead us into being deceived (error) so we end up choosing sin (apostasy) rather than God's ways of truth and righteousness.

My people are destroyed for lack of knowledge... (Hosea 4:6)

Our enemy Satan does not want us to know or grow in our understanding of God's Word. He will lie and tell us we can't understand the Bible. But always remember the Holy Spirit is our teacher and God's word says His sheep <u>*will hear*</u> His voice (John 10:27).

God wants to speak to us more than we realize. He has many wonderful things He wants to reveal to us through His word. We can't even begin to imagine what God has prepared for our future!

That is what the Scriptures mean when they say, "No eye has seen, no ear has heard, and no mind has imagined what God has prepared for those who love him." (1 Corinthians 2:9) NLT

6. Take Time to Pray

Prayer is simply having a conversation with your heavenly Father. Like any parent that is concerned about their relationship with their child, the need for communication is important to them. God *knows all*, but wants you to *tell all...* of your concerns—questions and your troubles to Him.

As in any relationship, lack of communication is destructive. God wants communion with us. Here are some verses to encourage you in your prayer life with your heavenly Father.

(God says) **In those days when you pray, I will listen ...If you look for me in earnest, you will find me <u>when you seek me</u>. (Jeremiah 29:12-13) NLT**

In the day of my trouble I will call upon You, <u>For You will answer me</u>... Among the gods there is none like You, O Lord; Nor are there any works like Your works. (Psalms 86:7-8) NKJV

<u>Pray at all times</u> and on every occasion in the power of the Holy Spirit. Stay alert and be persistent in your prayers for all Christians everywhere. (Ephesians 6:18) NLT

We must make the choice to spend quality time with God each day in prayer. It is easy to put other things first in our lives. Our prayers are so important to God He saves them in containers in heaven as mentioned in this heavenly scene from the Book of Revelation:

> **Worthy Is the Lamb** Now when He had taken the scroll, the four living creatures and the twenty-four elders fell down before the Lamb, each having a harp, and golden bowls full of incense, which are the prayers of the saints. (Rev 5:8) NKJV

> But we have this treasure in jars of clay, to show that the surpassing power **belongs to God** and not to us.
> —2 Corinthians 4:7

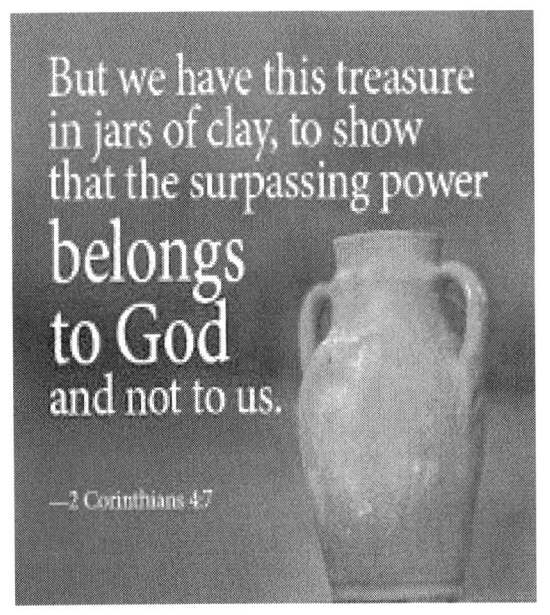

However, if you will develop the discipline of seeking God first each day, before your time is taken up with other things—you will be more prepared to handle the difficulties that are sure to come your way.

Nowhere in the Bible are we promised by God to have a <u>problem free life</u> when we choose to follow Jesus, (in fact quite the opposite), but God does promise to be there in the midst of it all. For His power dwells in us when we are truly born again.

> **Remember the word that I said unto you, the servant is not greater than his lord. If they have persecuted me, they will also persecute you... (John 15:20) KJV**

But this precious treasure — this light and power that now shine within us — is held in perishable containers, that is, in our weak bodies. So everyone can see that our glorious power is from God and is not our own... We are pressed on every side by troubles, but we are not crushed and broken. We are perplexed, but we don't give up and quit... We are hunted down, but God never abandons us. We get knocked down, but we get up again and keep going. (2 Corinthians 4:7-9) NLT

As I mentioned before, the Bible identifies King David as a *man after God's own heart.* When you read about his life, you will find that he was a man that loved God and wanted to honor Him with his life. He was a good king and did many great things for God's people. In fact, God promised David that it would be through his family line that Jesus would be born.

You will also find that David failed God greatly by falling into temptation and sin. His sin cost him dearly, but David never stopped loving or trusting God until the Day He died. David knew how to pray and praise God through it all.

Most of the Psalms in the Old Testament were written by him. Like David, we too must live a life of praising God by always reminding ourselves of how wonderful He is and how great His mercy and loving kindness towards us is.

Praise the LORD, I tell myself; with my whole heart, I will praise his holy name... Praise the LORD, I tell myself, and never forget the good things he does for me... He forgives all my sins and heals all my diseases... He ransoms me from death and surrounds me with love and tender mercies... He fills my life with good things. My youth is renewed like the eagle's! ...The LORD gives righteousness and justice to all who are treated unfairly. (Psalm 103:1-6) NLT

It is also good to speak out loud and declare what God shows us in His Word about what He wants to do for us, our families, our cities— nations and circumstances. This is what is known as a *prayer declaration.*

You will also declare a thing, and it will be established for you; So light will shine on your ways. (Job 22:28) NKJV

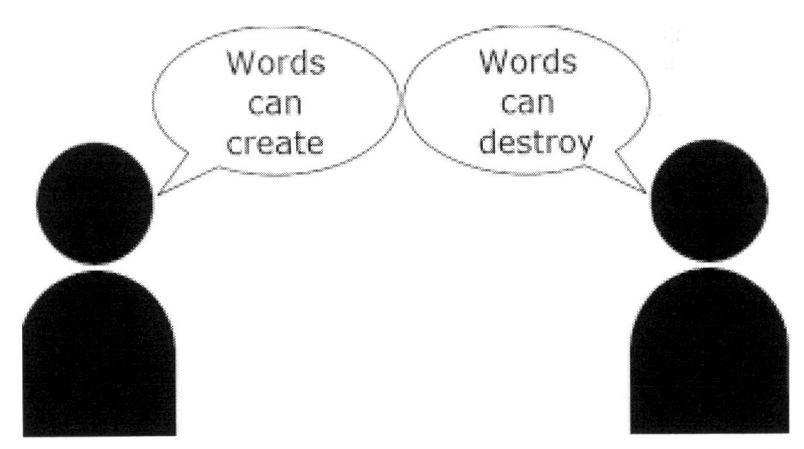

Words can create

Words can destroy

God's Word says there is the power of *life* or *death* in the words that we speak. God alone decides what will live or die. When we speak what God's has spoken to us—we are speaking words of faith. Faith gives life to God's will and to His promises (always keep in mind what we speak or declare must be His will and not our will). On the other hand, when we speak the fearful thoughts of the enemy that He speaks to us—we are speaking death over our concerns and desires from God. Here are some Scriptures that reveal the importance of what we speak.

<u>**Death and life are in the power of the tongue**</u>**, and those who love it** (i.e. speaking words) **will eat its fruit. (Proverbs 18:21) NKJV**

It is pleasant to listen to wise words, but <u>the speech of fools</u>

<u>**brings them to ruin**</u>. **(Ecclesiastes 10:12) NLT**

<u>**Then words of praise will be on their lips**</u>. **May they have peace, both near and far, <u>for I will heal them all</u>," says the LORD. (Isaiah 57:19) NLT**

Speaking out loud the truth revealed to us from God's word is a powerful weapon that saves and delivers us from fear, depression, sickness or anything people, the world or the devil may use against us. If we truly believe what the word of God has to say, we must speak it forth as an act of faith. The Bible says, faith without works is dead faith.

And since we have the same spirit of faith, according to what is written, "<u>I believed and therefore I spoke</u>," we also believe and therefore speak... (2 Corinthians 4:13) NJKV

Make it your practice to speak God's word over your life and circumstances. By <u>meditating upon the word of God</u> as you read it—the Holy Spirit will bring to you the Scriptures you need to declare for everything you must face.

Blessed is the person whose delight and desire are in the precepts, the instructions, the teachings of God; he habitually meditates, ponders and studies, by day and by night. (Ps 1:2) AMP

The Bible says God's word is the *sword of truth*. It is the only offensive weapon we have been given to fight against the devil and his lies. Satan can do us no harm unless we believe his lies. That is why he trembles at the word of God, which is the truth that will expose his lies which destroys his power over our lives.

Speaking the word is powerful and is essential in fighting the good fight of faith. For example, you can declare the word of God over your life by simply declaring Scriptures like these when you pray...

Father in Heaven... I thank you because I am your child, and (1 John 4:3-4) says I have a greater power within me than any spiritual power the devil can use against me! I thank you for your promise in (Hebrews 13:5) that says you will never leave me or forsake me. I praise you because Your word declares in (Isaiah 49:16) that you have my name written on the palm of your hand! I thank you that I never need worry about having my needs met because you have promised me in (Philippians 4:19) that you will meet all of my needs according to your riches in glory.

I will not fear the future because (Jeremiah 29:11) says you have it all worked out for me! And (Philippians 4:13) promises me that you will strengthen me... Therefore, I declare that I can do all the things You have planned for me to do!! Amen

Developing the habit of declaring God's word this way is your mighty and exceedingly powerful weapon called the sword of the Spirit, which is part of your armor given to you by God that is to be used against the devil and his evil influences—on your journey through this life with Jesus Christ! When you read a verse from the Bible that speaks to your heart—write it down and use it when you pray.

And take the helmet of salvation, and the <u>sword of the Spirit, which is the word of God</u>. (Ephesians 6:17) KJV

Developing the habit of declaring what God's word has spoken to you is your mighty and exceedingly powerful weapon against the devil and his evil influences while on your journey through this life with Jesus Christ! This means:

No weapon formed against you shall prosper, and every tongue which rises against you in judgment You shall condemn. This is the heritage of the servants of the LORD, and their righteousness is from Me," Says the LORD. (Isa 54:17) NKJV

> People will hurt you, God will heal you. People will humiliate you. God will magnify you. People will judge you. God will justify you. Just Have Faith.

CHAPTER 4

The Bible

The Bible is truly the most remarkable book ever written. It is a compilation of sixty-six books written by 40 men from 1500 B.C. to about 100 A.D. Although these men lived at various times and in various places and were from various backgrounds—there is no contradiction found among their writings, instead there is a complete harmony and continuity among their writings. This is because the same mind (of God) was at work in all of their books.

No other book ever written has displayed this supernatural unity and harmony among so many contributors to one volume of writings. It has been reported for about 50 years now that the Bible has been the largest seller of all books published in the history of the world!

Many people wonder which ***translation*** of the Bible they should read. Some translations are better than others. Because as I mentioned in the previous chapter, we must understand that the original *Bible* known as the *cannon of Scripture* was written in the *Hebrew, Aramaic and Greek* languages.

I believe God chose these languages specifically because of how expressive they are. It is from these original languages then, that ALL Bible translations exist. The Hebrew Bible was written by the Hebrew people 2,500 to 3,500 years ago. Their culture and lifestyle were very different than our own western culture.

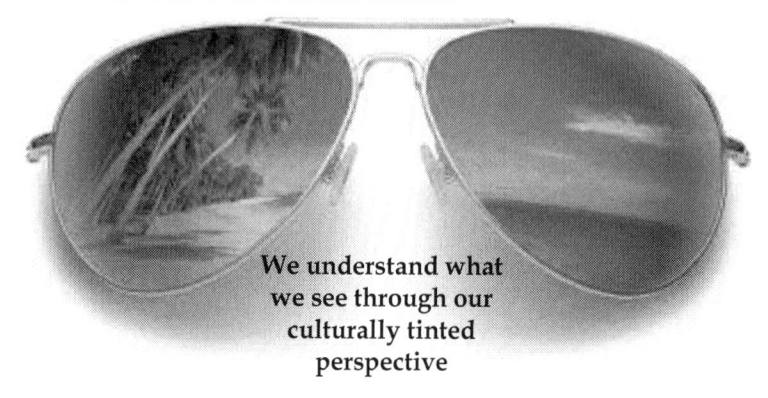

We understand what we see through our culturally tinted perspective

When we read the Word of God as a 20th Century American for example, our culture and lifestyle often influence our interpretation of its words and phrases. That is why we need to understand the Bible in the *original languages* that God chose for them to be written in. It is for this reason that I use various translations in my teaching ministry—in order to best convey my point in a way that is closest to what the original languages are saying.

There is no one single translation that has been able to capture all of the different shades of meanings that are expressed in the original Hebrew and Greek texts.

Many times our 20th century culture can influence definitions of words that were not intended by the original author. For example, the Bible often refers to *keeping* and *breaking* God's commands and covenant. The phrase *"to keep"* the commands of God—is usually interpreted and understood as to *"obey"* the commands, but this is not a complete understanding—because the phrase *to keep* is the Hebrew word "***shamar***" which literally means *to guard* or *protect*. Likewise, the phrase *"breaking of the commands"* is usually understood as *"disobeying"* them—but the Hebrew word is "***Parar***" and it literally means to *trample underfoot*.

Thus, one can see that *disobeying* or *breaking God's* word more accurately implies *an* act of disrespect. When we *break* God's commandments we are *trampling His Word under our feet.*

You can rest assured that God has seen to it that His Word (the Bible) has been preserved exactly as He has wanted us to have it and that everything which God has said in His word will be fulfilled and also accomplish what He has intended for His Word to do...

Then said the LORD unto me, you have well seen: for I will <u>hasten</u> my word <u>to perform it</u>. (Jeremiah 1:12) KJV

The word ***hasten*** in the above verse, according to the *New Exhaustive Strong's Dictionary,* is the Hebrew word ***al-shaqad*** (al-shaw-kad'). According to the Hebrew definitions—this word can also be translated *alert,* or *to* <u>watch over.</u> So God is saying through the prophet Jeremiah that He *personally watches over* His words *which he has communicated to us.* The *Amplified Version* translates the word *hasten* (as used in the *King James Version)*—as to <u>watch over</u>...

Then said the Lord to me, you have seen well, for I am alert and active, <u>watching over</u> My word to perform it. (Jeremiah 1:12) AMP

Thus we can see that God says He <u>watches over His word,</u> which means He has seen to it that it will be preserved and <u>never pass away.</u>

Heaven and earth will pass away, but My words will by no <u>means pass away</u>. (Luke 21:33) NKJV

Either we choose to believe that God is all powerful as the Bible says He is—or He is not. When we choose to believe He is all powerful, then we must also believe that He is more than able to make sure His word is free from error and has been (and will be) preserved for all generations.

The Accuracy of the Bible

The original written manuscripts of the Bible have been lost. But before they were lost, they were copied. These copies or manuscripts were incredibly accurate, very meticulous, and very precise. The people who copied them were called Scribes and were extremely dedicated to God and their copying tasks.

They took great care when copying the original manuscripts. This copying method is so exact, and so precise, that the New Testament alone is considered to be 99.5% *textually* pure.

THE BIBLE MAY HURT YOU WITH THE TRUTH BUT IT WILL NEVER COMFORT YOU WITH A LIE.

This means that of the 6000 Greek copies (the New Testament was written in Greek), and the additional 21,000 copies in other languages, there is only one half of 1% variation. Of this very slight number, the great majority of the variants are easily corrected by comparing them to other copies that don't have the *"typos"* or by simply reading the context.

The copying mistakes that occurred were things like word repetition, *spelling,* or a single word omission due to the copyist missing something when moving his eyes from one line to another. For this reason, the variants or *copying errors* are very minor and in no way affects the *historical accuracy, doctrinal truths* or the *words and deeds of Christ*—which have been unquestioningly free from error and reliably transmitted to us. The Bible is so exceedingly accurate in its transmission from the original manuscripts to the present copies, that if you compare it to any other ancient writing, the Bible is light years ahead in terms of number of manuscripts and accuracy. If the Bible were to be discredited as being unreliable, then it would be necessary also to discard the writings of—Homer, Plato, and Aristotle as being unreliable—since they are far, far less well preserved than the Bible.

The Inspiration of the Bible

The Bible was written by those who were *inspired by God*, therefore, it is accurate and true, and reveals many historical events and occurrences. When we look at the New Testament we realize that it was written by those who either knew Jesus personally, or were under the direction of those who did.

They wrote what they saw. They wrote about the resurrection of Christ. They recorded His miracles and His sayings. It comes down to whether or not you believe or have faith in what it says about Christ.

In The book of Revelation God is seen opening *the books* on judgment day. These *books* are the *sixty six books of the Bible*... from which all mankind will be judged...

And I saw the dead, small and great, stand before God; and the books were opened (the Bible): and another book was opened, which is the book of life: and the dead were judged out of those things which were written in the books (the Bible), according to their works. (Revelation 20:12) KJV (parenthesis mine)

God is a just God, therefore He will *watch over His word* to make sure His word remains as he intended it to be... *the whole truth and nothing but the truth*—from which we will be judged.

Any who change or pervert God's Word—by *adding to it* or *taking away from it*—their names will not be found in the book of life. Many false teachers and preachers are doing this very thing. They are in for a horrible shock when they stand before God in their time of judgment!

For I testify to everyone who hears the words of the prophecy of this book: If anyone adds to these things, God will add to him the plagues that are written in this book; ...and if anyone takes away from the words of the book of this prophecy, God shall take away his part from the Book of Life, from the holy city, and from the things which are written in this book. (Revelation 22:18-19) NKJV

God is saying that when we change His word by reading things into it that are not there—our names will not be found in the *Book of Life*. We can see why the ancient scribes were perfectionists when it came to transcribing the ancient manuscripts. If the *tiniest error* was detected in a completed manuscript, it was destroyed and redone.

By all of this one can see why using a Bible dictionary to help understand word meanings is crucial. It not only expands our understanding of the original word meanings but it also helps to make sure the *original text* is being accurately conveyed and understood by us. Some Bible translations are completely inaccurate, because they pervert the foundational doctrines of Christianity, such as the deity and *true identity* of Jesus Christ.

Any translation of Scripture which denies that *Jesus Christ is and always has been Jehovah God*, or teaches that salvation is obtained any other means apart from faith in His shed blood, is teaching false doctrine...

1 But there were also false prophets among the people, even as there will be false teachers among you, who will secretly bring in destructive heresies, even denying the Lord who bought them, and bring on themselves swift destruction. 2 And many will follow their destructive ways, because by whom the way of truth will be blasphemed. 3 By covetousness they will exploit you with deceptive words... (Peter 2:1-3) NKJV

To believe that the Bible was inspired by God, we must have faith that the perfect true and living God inspired imperfect people to write what he breathed into their soul. Listen to what God says through the writer of the book of Job...

But there is a spirit in man, And the breath (inspiration) of the Almighty gives him understanding. (Job 32:8) KJV (Parenthesis mine).

The Bible states that God is the author of what he inspired man to write down as His Holy Scriptures. God would not be a JUST God if he didn't make sure we had access to the truth He requires us to know and live by...

<u>All scripture is given by inspiration of God</u>, and is profitable for doctrine, for reproof, for correction, for instruction in righteousness: That the man of God may be perfect, thoroughly furnished unto all good works. (2 Timothy 3:16-17) KJV

God inspires people to speak and write what He wants made known. If we do not believe that the Bible is God's standard for truth and that it is free from human error, *we have no foundation for truth*.

This means we have nothing to measure what we believe by. When this is the case we then become gods unto ourselves, determining truth according to what *we choose to think*.

That is exactly what Satan did, when he appeared to Eve in the Garden of Eden in the form of a serpent. He got her to determine what her foundation for truth would be—which was, *what she chose to believe*, rather than what God had spoken.

Satan convinced her, not to believe what God said (His word)—but instead believe what he said, by also convincing her that **......you shall be as gods... (Genesis 3:5)** especially when it comes to interpreting the Bible.

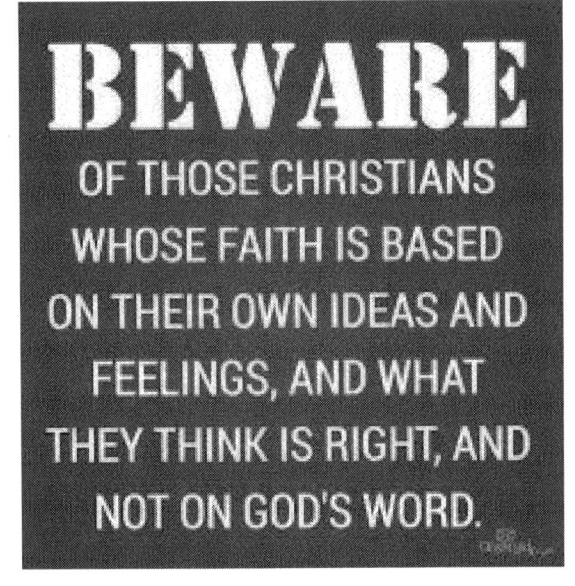

> **BEWARE** OF THOSE CHRISTIANS WHOSE FAITH IS BASED ON THEIR OWN IDEAS AND FEELINGS, AND WHAT THEY THINK IS RIGHT, AND NOT ON GOD'S WORD.

Getting the first humans on planet earth to doubt what God spoke is not only what Satan desired but it is also what he accomplished. Our faith as Christians must be in the fact that God's word is the **ONLY standard for truth** and that it is free *from error*. God is still speaking today through those who are able to *hear His voice*. All born again people can hear His Voice, and must choose to obey that voice.

My sheep hear My voice, and I know them, and they follow Me. (John 10:27) NKJV

As mentioned, the original Scriptures were written by humans who were *inspired* by what God spoke to them. Therefore, it takes the ability to hear God's voice when it comes to what *interpretation* we give to or receive from the Scriptures. God must also inspire the interpretation of His Word so it is correctly understood. When God speaks to us it is called *prophecy*. God through His Holy Spirit still speaks to us today—through His modern day prophets and He also speaks to us *when we read or study the Bible*.

Knowing this first, that no prophecy (what we hear God say) from Scripture is of any private interpretation... **for prophecy** (hearing God speak) **never came** (and still doesn't come) **by the will of man, but holy men of God speaking as they were moved** (inspired) **by the Holy Spirit.** (2 Peter 1:20-2:3) **KJV** (Parenthesis mine for clarity).

This means we cannot give the word of God our *private or personal* interpretation (explanation). Many try to twist the Scriptures to fit their personal opinions and ideas. As we just said, those who do this are putting their eternal destiny in jeopardy.

...the ignorant and unstable twist and misconstrue to their own utter destruction... by distorting and misinterpreting the rest of the Scriptures. (2 Peter 3:16) AMP

It is <u>only</u> through the <u>inspiration of God's Holy Spirit</u> that He explains the true meaning of His written word. As we meditate on the Scriptures He will reveal their true meaning.

However, when He, the Spirit of truth, has come, He will guide you into all truth... (John 16:13) NKJV

This is how those with the life and light of God within them—through the indwelling Holy Spirit—will be able to understand the Bible through God's inspiration, which is also called His *anointing*.

But you have an <u>unction</u> (anointing) from the Holy One, and you know all things... But the <u>anointing which you have received</u> of him abides <u>in you</u>, and you need not that any man teach you: but as the same <u>anointing teaches</u> you of all things, and is <u>truth</u>, and is no lie, and even as it hath taught you, you shall abide in him. (Because God's light is upon our spirit) **(1 John 2:20,27) KJV** (Parenthesis mine).

I pray you will take seriously God's command to study His word so you can become skilled in knowing the truth that will keep you free from all error and deception that is running rampant in many churches today. My prayer is that every true believer in Jesus Christ may learn to *rightly divide* God's Word of truth!

Study to show thyself approved unto God, a workman that needs not to be ashamed, rightly dividing the word of truth. (2 Tim 2:15) KJV

By doing this we will become skilled in faithfully handling the Word of God. This means we never need stand before our Lord at His judgment seat and feel ashamed, because we have mishandled or neglected to receive the truth from His Word. Those who stand before God and are approved by Him as His faithful workman, will hear these wonderful words spoken to them at the end of their life's journey...

'Well done, my good and faithful servant. You have been faithful in handling this small amount, so now I will give you many more responsibilities. Let's celebrate together!' (Matt 25:21) NLT

NOTES

NOTES

NOTES

ANATOMY FOR DECEPTION
If Possible Even the Very Elect Will be deceived!

Karen E. Connell

This Revised Edition is very timely!!
Request Your Free Copy
This book is an absolute *must* read for every sincere Christian who is wanting to remain free from deceptions that Have invaded many of the churches

Other Inspiring Resources
By
Karen Connell

NORMALIZING EVIL:
Through False Teaching

Karen E. Connell

NORMALIZING EVIL
Through false Teaching

This book explores how the melding of false teachings from various Christian movements have gained momentum through lying and seducing spirits that have been loosed upon the earth, in these end times—as prophesied in the Bible. The false teachers, doctrines and the pseudo worship associated with these deadly deceptions—are being seen and accepted as *normal* within many Christian circles and among multitudes of professing Christians. Karen, as a watchman from God—is sounding the alarm for all who have ears to hear concerning what is written within these pages. A call is being given to God's people to come out from among—all that is compromising and deceptive.

The Spiritual Gifts Manual

This course is FREE
Enroll now!

Manual may be requested without enrolling in the Spiritual gifts course

God has given every born again Christian spiritual gifts that are to be used as *tools* for doing the work of their ministry. Learn how to recognize your gifts and how to operate in them by enrolling in the Spiritual Gifts Course and by studying this manual. This is a very comprehensive study on this most important subject.

WOMEN IN MINISTRY

In this newly revised book, Karen shares a sound Biblical and historical perspective regarding the most misunderstood subject of **women in ministry.** Rather than allowing the Holy Spirit to reveal what the Bible has to say on this subject, far too many men and women have embraced false cultural and denominational viewpoints. The word of God, however, must be our final authority for all things—especially when it comes to fulfilling the call of God upon our lives as God's people. Satan has tried to disqualify women, through his *doctrines of demons,* from fulfilling their God ordained ministries. May men and women of God worldwide need to be set free from these false teachings and rise up and become all that God has called them to be!

Investigating and Experiencing The Glory of God

This booklet examines such things as:

- How the Bible defines the "glory" of God and it's purpose in our lives.
- Biblical patterns for God's true glory.
- True revival as well as true and false manifestations of God's glory.
- Keys for releasing God's glory through "true" worship.

Request Your FREE Copy of our Resource Catalog by filling out the order form on the following page

SPIRITUAL WARFARE

In this book I will be sharing some the insights and revelations the Lord has graciously given to me in order to keep me from following some of the popular false beliefs and practices related to spiritual warfare that are contrary to the Scriptures.

There is much being taught and written on the subject of *spiritual warfare*, but we must let the Word be the final authority on this topic.

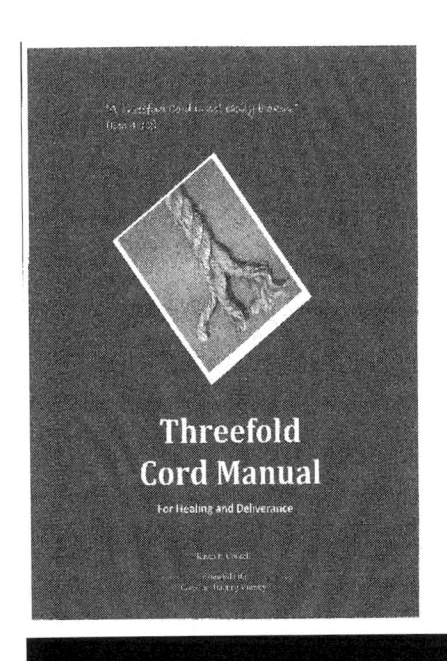

Threefold Cord Manual
For Healing and Deliverance

Three Fold Cord
Counseling Manual

It is important to have an understanding of how Satan and demons are able to wound and manipulate our fallen human nature, so that we end up struggling with their evil influences in our lives. This manual has led many into experiencing freedom and healing from Satan's power!

Enroll in these FREE courses By filling out the order form On the following page

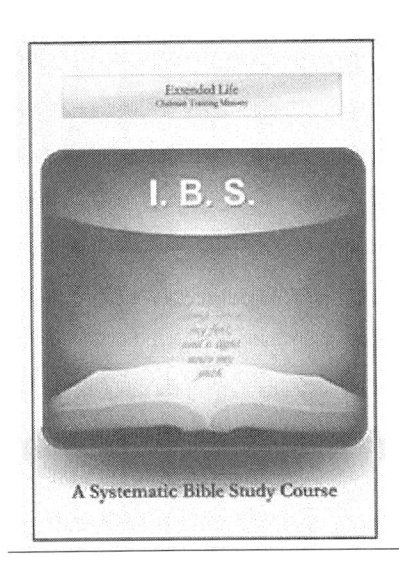

I.B.S.
A Systematic Bible Study Course

Internet Bible Study Course

Each lesson can be downloaded on line and is accompanied by an audio teaching that may be listened to on-line an mp3 file. Otherwise the lessons and audio CD teachings can be mailed if the course is taken as a correspondence course. Students will receive great insight into every book of the Bible through this material.

GOT A LIFE? It's a Gift from God   Karen E. Connell

Please complete this form to place an order by mail... For more resources by Karen Connell go to: **www.extendedlifeCTM.org** resource page

Name_____

Address_____

City_____ State_____ Zip_____

Phone ( )_____ e-mail_____

I have enclosed a love offering in the amount of $_____

☐ Please check if you would like to be placed on The TRUMPET SOUNDS Newsletter mailing list

How many FREE copies of the following you would like?

___ Copies of: the *Extended Life C.T.M.* **Resource Catalog**

___ Copies of: the latest issue of the **Trumpet Sounds Newsletter**

___ Copies of: **SPIRITUAL GIFTS Manual**

___ Copies of: **Women In Ministry**

___ Copies of: this months **NORMALIZING EVIL: Through False Teaching**

___ Copies of: **Threefold Cord Manual: Healing and Deliverance**

___ Copies of: this months **Investigating and Experiencing the Glory of God**

___ I would like information on enrolling in the following courses:
_____
_____
_____

There are no charges for these products or for our newsletter. *Any offering to help with production and mailing costs is always very much appreciated!* For those who have inquired regarding an offering Make checks payable to:
Karen E. Connell
734 W. Water St. Hancock, MI 49930

DISCOVER   MasterCard   VISA   AMERICAN EXPRESS

You may also use a credit card

Card Type_____

Card #_____

Name on card_____

Expiration Date_____

Made in the USA
Columbia, SC
27 September 2020